T0129090

Praise for *What Language Is*

"The King's English topples from the throne of linguistic legitimacy in this rollicking tour of human language. McWhorter unearths a wealth of colorful linguistic facts, from which he distills larger principles, couching his erudition in a lucid, supple prose. The result is a fascinating romp through the ornery wonders of language."

—*Publishers Weekly* (starred review)

"McWhorter walks through his five signal characteristics of language with a spring in his step and armed with a vast collection of interesting— and convincing—examples . . . *What Language Is* isn't another 'oh, that wacky language!' book; its mission is far broader than just to give a tour of other languages' customs and habits."   —*The Wall Street Journal*

"Energetic, brisk, and often amusing analysis of how language works."
—*The Columbus Dispatch*

"If there is something [John McWhorter] doesn't do well, we won't find it in his new work, *What Language Is.* . . . And speaking of prose style, this book is an example of the sort of writing everyone should aspire to. . . . While language is ubiquitous, written ones are a minority. This book is a reason to consider ourselves fabulously fortunate."

—*New York Journal of Books*

"Insightful . . . eye-opening, even liberating."   —*Kirkus Reviews*

"McWhorter boldly offers general readers another taste of language study. He presents a wealth of examples of English dialects when considering matters of grammar. These will fascinate, as will the similar development of two imperial languages, English and Persian . . . the distinctive blend of detail, accessible tone, and solid research will appeal to language students of all kinds."   —*Library Journal*

HOLLY MCWHORTER

John McWhorter is a renowned linguist and the author of more than a dozen books, including *Our Magnificent Bastard Tongue: The Untold History of English* and the *New York Times* bestseller *Losing the Race: Self-Sabotage in Black America*. He teaches linguistics and Western civilization at Columbia University, is a contributing editor at *The New Republic*, and has appeared widely in the media. He lives in New York.

ALSO BY JOHN MCWHORTER

WHAT LANGUAGE IS

(AND WHAT IT ISN'T AND
WHAT IT COULD BE)

JOHN MCWHORTER

GOTHAM
BOOKS

GOTHAM BOOKS
Published by Penguin Group (USA) Inc.
375 Hudson Street, New York, New York 10014, U.S.A.

Penguin Group (Canada), 90 Eglinton Avenue East, Suite 700, Toronto, Ontario M4P 2Y3, Canada (a division of Pearson Penguin Canada Inc.); Penguin Books Ltd, 80 Strand, London WC2R 0RL, England; Penguin Ireland, 25 St Stephen's Green, Dublin 2, Ireland (a division of Penguin Books Ltd); Penguin Group (Australia), 250 Camberwell Road, Camberwell, Victoria 3124, Australia (a division of Pearson Australia Group Pty Ltd); Penguin Books India Pvt Ltd, 11 Community Centre, Panchsheel Park, New Delhi–110 017, India; Penguin Group (NZ), 67 Apollo Drive, Rosedale, Auckland 0632, New Zealand (a division of Pearson New Zealand Ltd); Penguin Books (South Africa) (Pty) Ltd, 24 Sturdee Avenue, Rosebank, Johannesburg 2196, South Africa

Penguin Books Ltd, Registered Offices: 80 Strand, London WC2R 0RL, England

Published by Gotham Books, a member of Penguin Group (USA) Inc.

Previously published as a Gotham Books hardcover

First trade paperback printing, August 2012

Gotham Books and the skyscraper logo are trademarks of Penguin Group (USA) Inc.

Copyright © 2011 by John McWhorter
Maps by George W. Ward

THE LIBRARY OF CONGRESS HAS CATALOGED THE HARDCOVER EDITION OF THIS BOOK AS FOLLOWS:
McWhorter, John H.
    What language is : and what it isn't and what it could be / John McWhorter.
        p. cm.
    Includes bibliographical references and index.
    ISBN 978-1-592-40625-8 (hc)   978-1-592-40720-0 (pbk)
    1. Language and languages—Etymology.   2. Linguistic change.   3. Historical linguistics.
I. Title.
    P321M39 2011
    400—dc22   2011010208

Set in ITC Stone Serif Std • Designed by Sabrina Bowers

146122990

To those who disagreed with me,
and to Lara (1996–2010)

CONTENTS

INTRODUCTION

Page through a grand old book on what was once known as natural history—as we all do so often, of course—and you'll find that almost all drawings of marine life are rendered from the perspective of someone standing on the shore.

There will be some fish bobbing around out in the waves, and maybe some flying fish doing what they do. But clams, squid, sea anemones, and such will be lying on the beach, or artfully positioned on conveniently placed rock formations, or even just dangling from the margins of the picture. This was standard procedure in illustration until past the middle of the nineteenth century.

It all looks nice enough. But wouldn't it seem more natural to draw a squid swimming in the water, springy, fierce, and alert, instead of putrifying on a rock?

But then, what was "natural" to someone in 1840? Even if they were a naturalist? One thing that wasn't natural, if you think about it, was imagining what an underwater scene looked like—for a simple reason. People then didn't have the technology to ever *be* underwater for very long, and certainly not to be able to see much while even making a stab at it.

There were no diving bells or submarines. You might take a deep breath, hold your nose, and dive under for a look, but water is often muddy and it's hard to see through it when it's moving.

Plus, you can only hold your breath for so long—and certainly not long enough to plunge a mile down and get a peep at anglerfishes and such.

In England, it was only after a home aquarium mania in the 1850s that people started to get a sense of what aquatic creatures looked like in life, such that illustrators began drawing underwater marine scenes. Before this, as modern as the British were in so many ways, even those with advanced educations, three names, and salad forks had no way of picturing undersea life in the "Jacques Cousteau" style that is second nature to us. To start thinking of sea creatures that way, you had to see them that way.

And in many ways, quite often, to be a linguist is to feel like you're underwater in 1840 while everybody else is up on the beach laying jellyfish out on rocks.

IT'S BECAUSE SO MUCH about language is so hard to see. Or hear.

So from what it's easy to see and hear, we learn that there are languages, and then in many parts of the world there are assorted "dialects." These "dialects" are, in some sense, lesser than languages. Part of the difference would seem due to the fact that, as one typically supposes, a language is a collection of words. English has enough words to fill a doorstop like *The Oxford English Dictionary* (actually the printed version could practically serve as a garden wall). Some "dialect" out there in the rain forest does not—and therefore qualifies as something different from, well, a *language* language. And then there's the writing issue: if a language isn't fixed on the page, then surely, we suppose, it has not achieved its full power. A certain transiency hangs about it; it's just a "dialect," in other words.

Because of this it becomes natural that if asked which was more complex, French or the language of a tiny group in New Guinea called the Nasioi, most people would immediately suppose that the answer was French—a "developed" language, after all. The truth, however, begins with the observation that if you thought French's two genders were annoying, imagine having to deal with Nasioi's one hundred!

Down underwater, what we see is a world with six thousand languages, period, whether or not they ever see the printed page and even if their vocabularies number only in the tens of thousands. If anything, the languages that are a little "sub-ordinary," a little "special," as we might designate a certain congenitally ungifted sort of person, are typically rock-star ones like English, French, and Mandarin Chinese.

But who'd know? We'll never meet a Nasioi, much less have any reason to learn the language. Besides, we're too busy attending to other notions about our own language, such as that one of the gravest flaws of the Anglophone is a noisome propensity to use the language "illogically." We are taught that a language is sensible, tidy—such that we treat it as an oddity that English is shot through with random inconsistencies. Richard Lederer has heightened the festivity quotient of many an e-mail inbox via excerpts that get around from his *Crazy English* book along the lines of "Why are *loosen* and *unloosen* the same?" or "If we *conceive* a *conception* and *receive* at a *reception* why don't we *grieve* a *greption*?" or observations such as that there's no egg in eggplant and no ham in a hamburger.

This stuff is, in fact, but the tip of an iceberg of nonsensicality in English—underwater you can see the rest, but we humans are terrestrial. Not to mention territorial—don't even get most of us started on what happens when languages mix together. Spanish full of English words is "Spanglish," reviled by many and thought of as "an issue" by others. And there was even a time when more than a few had a serious problem with English having taken on so many words from French and Latin. After all, a *real* language is "pure."

HERE'S WHAT IT FEELS LIKE to be underwater.

One reads a perfectly pleasant newspaper article about people in the Caucasus Mountains, a patch of a region home to several dozen languages. The one closest to famous is Georgian. One of the other ones mentioned in the article, spoken by only about twelve hundred people in a few villages, is called Archi. And in the article, what do we learn about Archi? Only that it is a language "of unknown origin." Otherwise the article is about jokes Archi people and nearby Caucasian language–speaking groups tell about one another.

Of course I'm not waiting for a newspaper writer to give a linguistics lesson about Archi. But given the "on the beach" perspective on language that reigns, it's hard not to feel like something has happened when a language like this is flagged in passing, especially as some orphan. Attention must be paid—if not in the article, then somewhere. That "unknown origin" business, for example, with the quiet implication that as a kin-less sort of thing, Archi is all alone, as unclassable as it is unknown, outside of the light, less than something—a "dialect," perhaps?

To be sure, if the idea is that a language's "origins" must be on paper, then Archi is lost indeed—it has been a spoken language rather than a written one, like all but about two hundred of the world's six thousand languages. But paper isn't the only way to tell where a language came from.

A group of similar languages, such as French, Spanish, Italian, Portuguese, and Romanian, begin as one language, which splits off into several when populations become separated over time. Linguists can compare the word for something in related languages and deduce what that word was in the parent language. We know that the method works pretty well in cases where even the parent language was written down for posterity. For example, *hand* is *main* in French, *mano* in Spanish and Italian, *mão* in Portuguese, and *mână* in Romanian. No linguist is surprised, based on the techniques of what is called comparative reconstruction, that the Latin word for *hand* is *manus*.

In the same way, Archi is one of a passel of kittens, a language family called Northeast Caucasian. If the word for, say, *tongue* is *mac* in Archi—which it is—and *mott* in Chechen (the

one language of this family whose speakers are today known to the outside world), *maz* in Lak, *mez* in Lezgian, *mic* in Bezhta, *mott'* in Batsbi, *muz* in Udi, and *mici* in Tindi and so on, then linguists can use these words to roll back the tape and see that the original word in the parent language was *maʒi*, even though that language was never written down.

So Archi is not of "unknown origin" at all—it has kin, sprung from a *paterfamilias* language probably spoken about six thousand years ago. If anything, it is of better-known origin than most of us are as people. Most of us have no records of our ancestors further back than four or five generations and certainly couldn't reconstruct them from our DNA and our relatives'. The world is bursting with language families of this kind, whose ancestral languages can be reconstructed in the same way as the Caucasian word above. In some cases the ancestral languages can be shown to possibly be related to one another.

Or, while we're on "tongue"—the newspaper writer is hardly the first person to write of languages of the Caucasus with a subtle sense that they have not quite "arrived" in the sense that, say, German has. The grand old author of language books for the general public, Mario Pei, though a god of mine, repeatedly termed the Caucasus languages "tongues," as opposed to the "languages" he refers to elsewhere. "Among the widespread languages, Arabic is the one having the greatest variety of guttural sounds; but the tongues of the Caucasus are generally conceded to be the ones having the richest assortment of consonant-sounds," he had it. Or, in the very first issue of the flagship journal of linguistics, *Language*, wouldn't you know that one of the articles was titled "The Influence of Caucasian Idioms on Indo-European Languages." Mind you, the writer here did not mean "idiom" in the sense of *kick the bucket* or "What*ever*!" but just as a speech variety different from a language such as an Indo-European one. Spoken by small numbers of people often pre-literate until recently and almost never written down—surely these are tongues, idioms. And whatever those are, it's something different from a language.

That plays into the on-the-beach view of language—Archi, as it were, drying out on some piece of driftwood. But what a marvel is Archi when you can see it alive! For one thing, while English has a couple dozen consonants, Archi has over seventy-five! Just enunciating this "tongue" would leave most of ours in knots. And Pei even slipped a bit in designating Caucasian consonantal richness a world record: the Khoi-San "click" languages of southern Africa, also obscure and unwritten, are the ones with the biggest consonant inventories on earth. Pei squeezed by this with "The Hottentot-Bushman languages of southwest Africa use grunts and clicks as normal parts of their speech-sounds," apparently thinking that the "grunts and clicks" are not consonants. But they are, as central in indicating meaning as *b* and *h* are in distinguishing a bat from a hat: for example, the symbols ! and | indicate certain click sounds, and in the Nama click language of Namibia, *!hara* means "examine" while *|hara* means "dangle." But at least Pei, for some reason, called these "tongues" languages—and in any case, Archi is vastly richer in sounds than what an English speaker has any reason to think of as normal.

And then Archi's grammar steams and jangles with so much more "stuff" than English that it can be hard to imagine that people actually speak it casually, courting and cooking and dozing off in it, as opposed to the occasional gifted adolescent being sequestered to spend decades mastering it as a stunt to show off at festivals.

The following chart shows *When they were going up to Tura, they saw a bear* in Archi. The translation of each word is lined up underneath, with dashes between roots and their prefixes and suffixes. The double letters mean that you pronounce the consonant with special vigor. The double letter alone makes a difference in words' meanings just like *b* and *h* in *bat* and *hat*—χ*at* is "scratch" but χχ*at* is "beam."

Tura-li-ši	jatti-ši	χa(b)tti-ttib
Tura-in-to	upwards-to	went towards (they)-they
χχams	b-akku-li	jijme-s
bear	it-saw-"I heard"	they-to

The word order comes out as "Tura to up going they, bear saw by them," but that's just the beginning. The word for *went* has a *they* shoved right in the middle of it—*they* is just one sound (!), *b*, and χatti becomes χa(b)tti, as if in English we said not "they travel" but "tra-they-vel." Then χatti is an irregular form, and not just for *went* but something more specific, what I translated as "went towards": as we have *went* for *go* in the past, Archi has an irregular *go* form for when the going hasn't finished yet and is just *towards* the end, a shade of meaning that verbs take suffixes for just as they do for pastness (and of course the ordinary past form of *go* is irregular, too!). And then you have to have *they* yet again, as the -*ttib* at the end—but that is a form that you use only in a subordinate clause!

And in real life χa(b)tti-ttib isn't uttered with helpful parentheses and dashes: it just goes by in a flash—χabttittib—and as part of a sentence, not on display by itself, and nobody puts spaces between words when they talk, so—*Turališijattišiχabttitti bχχamsbakkulijijmes* . . . and that's just one sentence in a whole story! And in case you were wondering, χ is made by trilling your uvula—which sounds a little less exotic if compared to the similar gurgly *r* in French, but still.

A "tongue" indeed—and never mind that (get your uvula ready again) if the word χχams for *bear* were a subject, then often it would need a special ending, or that those endings are highly irregular, or that what I marked as "I heard" is a suffix that indicates that it's something you heard rather than experienced—and you have to use it.

And finally, there's so much irregularity in Archi that the

rules almost seem like the exceptions. The plural marker in English is -*s*. But from these words, can you tell what the plural marker is in Archi?

	singular	**plural**
pea	čak	čakmul
cheek	eχˤ	eχˤut
knee	poˤmp	poˤt
claw	χχeč	χχečum
potato	qʷˤib	qˤobor

Me either. Sure, we have *man* and *men*—but in Archi those are *bošor* and *kɬele*! Yet this is a mere humble "idiom"—in which, between verb prefixes and suffixes plus a breathtaking muchness else, a verb can occur in 1,502,839 different forms. To those of us underwater, reading an article highlighting Archi as what people tell jokes in is like watching someone get a prize for building a card house out of little paintings that are, despite no one considering it worthy of mention, Titians.

IT'S NOT ONLY THE OBSCURE "TONGUES" that harbor so much more than meets the eye (or ear), but ones more familiar, such as English. A language is a fecund, redolent buzzing mess of a thing, in every facet, glint, and corner, even in single words. For our purposes, let's take that word *idiom* as in the "Caucasian idioms." A bread-and-butter etymology like "From the Greek *idioma*, 'peculiarity, peculiar phraseology'" is fine, but there's more.

Just as we know that Northeast Caucasian's word for *tongue* was *maǯi*, from comparing words in the Romance, Germanic, and Slavic languages, plus Lithuanian, Irish and Welsh, Greek, Albanian, Armenian, Hindi, Persian, and plenty of others, we know that there was once a single ancestor to all of these languages in which a word for *self* was *swe*. Or better, *swe-*, because that language, which we call Proto-Indo-European, was very heavy on suffixes, and we can assume that *swe* came dressed in them much of the time.

Now, one of the most easily perceived ways that *swe* comes down to us is in that little *se* word that pops up in French, Spanish, and the gang in reflexive constructions, still meaning "self." Recall: French *Il se lave* or Spanish *Él se lava*, "He washes himself." For the record it's also where our own *self* comes from, with an antique suffix frozen on, the meaning of which has been long lost.

In other cases, *swe* wended down different paths we'd never think of now. If you're by yourself or within yourself, you're apart from others, and that was the meaning of a *swe* rendition in Latin, *sed*, with the *w* dropped out and another one of those suffixes, -*d*, stuck on: "apart." Hence when *sed* joined with *cura*, "care," as in "worry," the result was *sed-cura* "apart from worry," which became *securus*, which English inherited as *secure*.

In Greek, *swe* went its own "separate" way. Your self is particular to you, such that the *swe* rendition *swed* (with another one of those mysterious frozen suffixes) took on that connotation. But not quite in that form. For one thing, Proto-Indo-European made *swed* into an adjective with a -*yo* suffix, and thus *swed-yo*, "self-ic," as it were. And then there was a Greek "particularity"—*s* and *w* at the beginning of words had a way of flaking off, like *h* did in many regional British varieties (*'orse*, *'ouse*, and so on). That's why the Proto-Indo-European root *sreu*, "flow," lives on in English as *stream*, but in Greek as the *s*-less *rhythmos* (the source of our *rhythm*), and it's why the root *werg* became *work* in English but in Greek became *organon* (with no *w*)—and thus words like *organic* in English.

This meant that *swedyo* became the Greek word *edyo* and before long, with the "eh" sound changing to an "ee" as it often does in languages over time, *idio*. One result: a person with a plethora of particular qualities may possibly be a weirdo, and there's a short step from weirdo to *idiot*. But then another result: one thing particular to a person could be their language, especially as language is so deeply tied to psychology and identity. Naturally, then, *idio* could start to refer to one of the most particular particularities of being human, one's *idiom*. The *m* began as the first sound in one of Greek's first-person-singular endings, à la Spanish's *-o* in *hablo*, "I speak": *idiou-mai* meant "I make my own." Latin took that on as *idioma*, but as a noun, with the *m* having no meaning of its own. Then English borrowed that, and never gave it back.

Which means, though, that *idiom* is the tail end of an imperceptibly gradual process of change in sound, meaning, and suffixation, such that the first *i* is all that's left of the original *swe*—the *sw-* flaked off and the *e* morphed into an *i*. The *d* is the remnant of that ancient Proto-Indo-European suffix, the *io* of that other one that used to make a noun into an adjective and is now just a glide of the tongue, and the *m* is left over from a chunk of Greek we English speakers wouldn't recognize as a suffix if it bit us on the leg.

That's how words are in any language. Good old *swe*, for the record, is also frozen into **su**llen (how you might feel when you're by your*self*), **ethnic** (that is, your *own* people—with that Greek *sw-* lost again), and *boat***swain** (the swain is "your *own* man" up there on the boat). It's even in the Irish organization name Sinn Fein, and not the *Sinn* but the *Fein*. The name means "We Our*selves*"—Proto-Indo-European *w*, as in *swe*, became *f* in Irish, which is why *werə-o-*, "true," became Latin's *vir*, "man" (source of English's *virile*), but is *fíor* in Irish today. *Swe* is even fossilized like an insect in amber in **sober**—Latin's *sed*, "apart," again, plus *ebrius*, familiar to us from *inebriated*, and thus "not drunk" was *sed ebrius*, "apart from drunk." Later *sed ebrius* merged into *sebrius* . . . and then vowels fidgeted over time as always, and so *sobrius*, and you can imagine the rest.

And that's just the spawn of *swe*. Every word we utter—within unbroken strings like *Turališijattišiχabttittibχχamsbakkul ijijmes*, all day every day, carries baggage from merry morphing just as *idiom* does. The way this morphing happens shows that language is a very different thing than it tends to seem.

Namely, in honor of the word *idiom* and its muttly history, with individual sounds tracing to different sources, I'd like to split the word up in a similar way so that it can show us the nature of human language more directly. In this book we will see that language, whether a "language," "tongue," or "idiom," is:

I: *Ingrown.* All speech varieties have to indicate things that are pretty obvious even if left unmentioned. The "tongues," however, have a navel-gazing way of taking this further than English speakers would imagine. Archi and its "I heard" marker is an example, as is the fact that if you do something to a bear it's a χχ*ams*, but if the bear does something to someone or something it's a χχ*amssi*. In fact, unwritten languages tend to be especially ingrown, because the big-dude globe-striding languages have usually been streamlined by earnest but semicompetent adults learning them out of necessity, unable to do it as well as they could have as children. If Archi were spoken by countless millions instead of a count-ful twelve hundred, it would probably be a lot less dazzlingly complicated.

D: *Dissheveled.* All speech varieties are messy, full of illogical things that Richard Lederer could write books about and then some. Archi plurals are crazier than *person* versus *people* as often as not. Or, another *sed-* story: Latin for "to separate" was *cernere*. *Sed + cernere,* "to separate apart," became *secernere,* from whose participial form *secretus* English got *secret.* Note that "separate apart" was the kind of thing that would be decried in Comments sections today as "redundant," like *irregardless* with its *ir-*, and yet it was the source of a word now considered quite correct. Quests to make language usage "logical" look, from underwater, quizzical given that all languages are, at heart, jerry-rigged splotches doing the best they can despite countless millennia of unguided, slow-but-sure kaleidoscopic distortion.

I: *Intricate.* Despite the kaleidoscopic accretions and destructions, anything a human being speaks is a coherent system with rules, unless the human being is a toddler, brain damaged, or making their way in a foreign language. This is even true of speech varieties deeply marked by adult learning, such as Black English, created by adult slaves making their way in English by hook or crook and never mastering some of the rules of Standard English. In Black English, new rules have been born that make Black English more like Archi in some ways than the language *The Wall Street Journal* is written in. Rules are about much more than tables of endings and issues about whether something is a subject or an object.

O: *Oral.* A speech variety is not primitive just because no one writes it. Writing is merely a scratching down of what speaking sounds like, and the speaking is ingrown, dissheveled, and intricate just as the written reflection of it is. The now common concern about the looseness of writing online and in texting is a distraction born of an "onshore" perspective on what a language is. Writing is not "the language" itself, and how someone writes an e-mail has nothing to do with the marvelous complexity of how the same person talks, channeling their inner Archi in whichever language they speak. This, in turn, shows the fallacy in the alarm at speech increasingly coloring how we write. What has been strange is the separate development of writing from speech, and the blending of the two that modern communications technology allows is, in its way, creating a less artificial culture of language worldwide.

M: *Mixed.* "Pure" languages don't exist. Likely as many humans speak more than one language as do not, and in the same mouth, languages are no more likely to stay separate than two liquids. As former members of the Soviet Union, Archi speakers learn Russian in school and use it as the main language of communication with people beyond the twelve hundred Archis. As such, they are unlikely to speak Archi for longer than a few minutes without using a Russian word, just as Latin speakers used Greek words like *idiom* and English speakers started taking so many of those same words from Latin for themselves. Linguists have encountered no language that isn't penetrated with words, and even grammatical constructions, from other languages. Some readers will recall my showing in *Our Magnificent Bastard Tongue* that English's use of *do* in questions and negative sentences—*don't you know?*—is a steal from Celtic languages like Welsh.

AT THE CLOSE OF his *On the Origin of Species*, Charles Darwin famously wrote after his argument for natural selection as the source of the variety of the world's animals and plants:

> There is grandeur in this view of life, with its several powers, having been originally breathed into a few forms or into one; and that, whilst this planet has gone cycling on according to the fixed law of gravity, from so simple a beginning endless forms most beautiful and most wonderful have been, and are being, evolved.

In the same way, there is grandeur in this view of language. How and why human language emerged is hotly disputed, but we know that at some point it happened, as "so simple a beginning." And today we have "endless forms most beautiful and most wonderful." Not a few "languages" and a bunch of evanescent, rootless "idioms," but six thousand awesomely ingrown, messy, intricate, oral, and mixed creations.

To get a sense of what I mean, allow me to show you what the languages of the world look like from down here underwater.

CHAPTER ONE

LANGUAGES ARE INGROWN

I t was one of those times when the rain started falling so suddenly and so hard it was almost scary. An elderly man who had been out walking knocked on my screen door, soaked and desperate to get indoors somehow. He was staying with my next-door neighbors and had forgotten to bring his key. He didn't know when his family would be getting home.

What do you talk about with a complete stranger who ends up in your company for what is likely to be a long time? Especially when he turns out to be of only limited fluency in English? Well, when you're a linguist, one ready topic is the person's native language. His, as it turned out, was Persian.

THAT'S REALLY *IT*?

This was a good long time ago; I didn't know anything about Persian back then. So I started by asking him how to do a present-tense verb. He wrote out on a piece of paper:

I buy	mi-xar-**am**
you buy	mi-xar-**i**
he, she, it buys	mi-xar-**ad**
we buy	mi-xar-**im**
you folks buy	mi-xar-**id**
they buy	mi-xar-**and**

Okay, fine. Just the sort of thing you would expect—endings, and six of them as usual. Usual, that is, in Indo-European languages, as Persian is, like Spanish, German, and Russian. The *Indo-* part of Indo-European refers to, for one, most of India's languages, but also to those in Iran and thereabouts. Persian is

one, and so if in Spanish *buy* conjugates as *compro, compras, compra, compramos, compráis, compran*, then Persian's version is clearly akin. The Persian suffixes even look a little like their Spanish equivalents here and there.

But then I asked the man how to do the past conjugation, and that's where things got a little odd.

Here's what he gave:

I bought	xar-**id-am**
you bought	xar-**id-i**
he, she, it bought	xar-**id**
we bought	xar-**id-im**
you folks bought	xar-**id-id**
they bought	xar-**id-and**

Now, wait a minute. That's it?

There's always a single suffix *-id* that means just pastness, and then you just tack on the same endings from the present? Doesn't that, well, make a little too much sense?

It seems like it—given that you almost never get a break like this in the past tense in a typical Indo-European language. In Spanish, for example, you have:

I bought	compr-**é**
you bought	compr-**aste**
he, she, it bought	compr-**ó**
we bought	compr-**amos**
you folks bought	compr-**asteis**
they bought	compr-**aron**

No one piece of these suffixes means "past" all by itself like Persian's *-id*. Plus, in general they're confusing. The only difference between present tense *compro*, "I buy," and past tense *compró*, "I bought," is the stress on the *-o* suffix, and then *compramos* means both "we buy" and "we bought." And never mind that in Persian, you don't even have a personal ending in the third person singular. Just *xar-id*.

And it seemed like pretty much everything the elderly man told me about Persian that afternoon was like this—almost too easy, as if he had made it up himself. After he left, I wondered whether he had actually grown up speaking an obscure language of Iran and only learned Persian later and never that well. Maybe he figured, reasonably, that I wouldn't be interested in some village "tongue" and that I wouldn't know the difference between his Persian and "real" Persian. Surely this ABC thing he had shared with me wasn't a normal language.

And it isn't. Based only on what this man wrote on a sheet-and-a-half of paper that day, I could have known some things about the history of that language—because normal Indo-European languages just don't come out that way.

WHY CAN'T YOU BE LIKE YOUR BROTHER PASHTO?

Normal is a language we hear mentioned rather often but rarely learn anything about: Pashto. Pashto straddles Afghanistan and Pakistan, as do the people who speak it, the Pashtun. However, Pashto has no relationship to Arabic and is only distantly related to Indian languages like Hindi. It is another one of the languages in that Iranian group, related to Persian as German is to English. Persian and Pashto's names come from the same root— Persian started as *Parsa* and Pashto as *Parsawā*—and the languages are spoken side by side in Afghanistan. The Dari that people speak there is a dialect of Persian.

Yet Pashto and Persian are very different things. If that man who came to my apartment had been a Pashtun and was trying to explain his language, we might still be there today.

This is because Pashto is much, much more complicated than Persian. Take the past tense (please!). In Pashto, for one thing, verbs are conjugated differently according to whether they are transitive (i.e., take an object, like *kick*) or intransitive (i.e., don't take an object, like *sleep*). Therefore, transitive *throw* and intransitive *fall* conjugate differently: my visitor would have required more than one slip of paper to get this across:

I threw	ačaw-**əl**-əm	I fell	**lwed**-əm
you threw	ačaw-**əl**-e	you fell	**lwed**-e
he threw	ačāwə	he fell	lwed-ə
she threw	ačaw-**ə**la	she fell	lwed-**ə**la
we threw	ačaw-**əl**-u	we fell	**lwed**-u
you folks threw	ačaw-**əl**-ə́y	you folks fell	**lwed**-əy
those guys threw	ačaw-**əl**	those guys fell	lwed-**əl**
those gals threw	ačaw-**ə**le	those gals fell	lwed-**ə**le

Basically, the transitive verbs' endings have a cognate to that Persian -*id*, -*əl*, while the intransitive ones don't. But that's just a rule of thumb: transitives take no -*əl* with *he*, and then in intransitives there *is* an -*əl* in the third person—usually, that is. And then, in Pashto, unlike in Persian, there are different endings for *he* and *she* in both the singular and the plural. And finally, what's in bold indicates where the accent is—and it differs between the two verb types. With the intransitive ones, usually you accent the verb itself—except in the third person.

Imagine learning that in a classroom, stumbling every time you needed to utter a verb, struggling to process online whether it's transitive or intransitive. Or, remember those wacky Archi plurals in the introduction? Well, here are some Pashto plurals:

bāṅu-**gān** "eyelashes"
lās-**una** "hands"
lew-**ān** "wolves"
xwl-**e** "mouths"
pišo-**gāne** "cats"
xwāx̌-**yāne** "mothers-in-law"
mlā-**we** "waists"

And that's not all of the endings possible, and these are *regular*! For example, the first ending -*gān* is for, and only for, masculine nouns that end in –*u and aren't living beings*!

On the other hand, in Persian you don't always even have to mark the plural at all. *We have guests*, you tell someone who calls at an inopportune moment. The Persian for that would be, with the verb coming at the end as it does in Iranian languages, "We guest have"—*Mā mehmān darim*. There is no plural ending on *mehmān* there—it's just *guest* (as if it were me answering the phone while that man was at my house, and come to think of it, someone actually did call). You *could* use the plural marker and say *Mā mehmān-hā darim*, but that means something explicit, like "We've got a bunch of people over" or "There are all *kinds* of people here," not just a simple statement that you have guests. That's odd for an Indo-European language. Imagine being taught that in French "We have children" is *Nous avons enfant*. Or, even, imagine saying in English about your two daughters and a son, "We have child."

And other than *hā*, Persian has only one other plural marker, or more like half of one, since it isn't used a whole lot. To make a plural in Persian, you need pay no mind to whether things are non-living or whether they end with -*u* or anything else. And as for things' gender, it's a non-issue because Persian doesn't have any!

Or, Pashto has four cases, and they are indicated not only with endings but with vowel changes (like English turns *take* into *took*). Here's what happens to the little adjective *pox* for *ripe*, with bold indicating stress again:

	singular	plural
nominative	pox	pāxə
with *by*	pāxə	pax**o**
with other prepositions	p**o**xa	pax**o**

This is as if in English we said *big car* but *boga cars* and talked about people being driven *by boog cars*.

But Persian's nouns and adjectives stay the same whatever case they're in.

And these things are just a sample. Throughout its entire system, Pashto dots more *i*'s and crosses more *t*'s than Persian—a lot more. Why do two languages of the same subfamily, spoken right next to one another, work so very differently?

THE PERSIAN CONVERSION

It's because Persian and Pashto have had very different histories. Persia, after all, was once the great Achaemenid empire, reigning over speakers of countless other languages, westward from modern-day Turkey on to the Black Sea's shore in Greece, southward to modern-day Egypt, and eastward to modern-day India as well as regions today contained in Afghanistan, Pakistan, Turkmenistan, Uzbekistan, and Tajikistan.

At the outset of that situation, Persian was a very different language than it is today, as different from modern Persian as Old English is from today's—and a lot more like Pashto. In fact, it was more like Pashto than Pashto: Old Persian had not two genders like Pashto but three, masculine, feminine, and neuter, as German and Russian still do today. Persian today has no case endings, but Old Persian had eight cases.

When King Darius boasted of his power in a flinty cuneiform inscription on a cliff face in Behistun, it was in a language that would present us with the same classroom challenge that Latin or Ancient Greek does. Old Persian was all about case endings, as we see in this excerpt where Darius proclaims that he is:

xšāyaθiya xšāyaθiy**ānām**	king **of** kings
xšāyaθiya Pārs**aiy**	king **in** Persia
xšāyaθiya dahy**ūnām**	king **of** countries
Vištāspahyā puça	son **of** Hystaspes

Old Persian also had the *big, boga, boog* kind of vowel alternations that Pashto still does today. That word *dahyūnām* for "of the countries" in the Darius inscription, for example, was *dahyāuš* in the vanilla form of just "country," *dahyušuvā* for "in the countries," and *dahyauvā* for "in the country." The relevant vowels in *dahyauvā* were different from those in vanilla *dahyāuš* solely in that the *a* was short and therefore didn't have the "‾" over it—yes, that made a crucial difference; normal languages are *mean*!

But the "king of countries" in the inscription was key to what eventually made the difference between Modern Persian and Pashto. The Persian empire was full of people speaking things other than Persian.

As it happened, beyond Persia itself in the empire, people were *not* speaking Persian. The empire's rulers had little interest in imposing the language on its subjects, and instead business was conducted in Aramaic, a Middle Eastern language related to Arabic and Hebrew that had become established as a widespread lingua franca in the Assyrian empire before the Persian reign. But within Persia itself, Persian was naturally the language of choice—and there was a constant influx of people from elsewhere in the empire. They spoke many different languages and needed to learn Persian to communicate with Persians, as well as with one another.

Darius himself, in another inscription, wrote about how work crews in Persia were multiethnic mixes of Babylonians,

Egyptians, Greeks, and others. Other tablets mention people from eastern Iran and India as well. Parties of people coming into Persia were two-and-a-half times the size of parties of people leaving. Foreigners were such a robust part of the mix in Persia that a Greek writer summed up what he saw as "Iranians living among barbarians."

The situation seems even to have left genetic evidence. There is a marker on the Y chromosome termed M17, which seems to correlate with the spread of Indo-European languages, robust in people from the Ukraine down through Iran and India, but skipping the Middle East, where Semitic languages like Arabic and Aramaic are spoken. However, there is one strange dropout: M17 is vastly rare in, specifically, western Iran, where the Persian empire's capitals were. Geneticists have only ventured speculations as to this seemingly random kink in the data. Interestingly, however, M17 is also rare among Middle Easterners. If people from that area relocated to western Iran in massive numbers—as the historical evidence suggests they did—then the M17 dropout in just that region is explained.

In terms of what all of this meant for the fate of Old Persian, the simple question is: what do you think happened to the likes of *dahyāuš—dahyušuvā—dahyauvā* when legions of grown-ups started learning it?

Kids can learn any language, fast and perfectly—obvious when immigrants' children grow up sounding indistinguishable from their American peers. The skill atrophies in adults, however. There are occasional exceptions, those who master a new language with barely a trace of an accent and fine idiomatic command in their thirties. However, they are just that— exceptions, blessed with inborn talent and a leaning towards persistence. Generally, an adult cannot learn a new language to the point of sounding native—and especially when they are never taught it formally and have no reason to speak it anywhere near perfectly.

Imagine, then, a construction worker in Persis, one of the empire's capitals, who was born speaking Greek but now lives his life in Persian, picking it up from people around him. This is antiquity, mind you, and so no one gives him a book to study from or lays out the conjugation patterns on a blackboard. Almost no one is literate, and school as we know it doesn't exist—for the vast majority of people, language is something you speak, not something written on a page that you approximate by speaking. Writing is a formal activity, carved into cliff faces and such. There is no broadcast media to keep the formal language in the mix as a model.

In this kind of context, our construction worker learns new *words* every day, but as to grammar, he gets a sense of how the nouns take case and the verbs conjugate—but only a sense. And this is how most of the people around him speak Persian. And after a while, these immigrants start having kids. The kids hear this broken Persian at a tender age. In a world like this, if a critical mass of people are speaking broken Persian, then over generations the very essence of what Persian is starts to change. Namely, it gets easier.

For an English speaker, for example, something always a nuisance in Spanish is how to say *like*. It comes out as that something "pleases to you": *I like apples* is *Me gustan las manzanas*, "to-me please the apples." It's a very *specified* thing about Spanish, attending to the technicality that while to eat something is to do something to it, to like it is to experience it—i.e., for something to happen *to you*. The way an English speaker would like it to go is something like *Yo gusto las manzanas*, to bring it into line with our way of rendering liking, a less *specified* way of putting it. It's a typical Spanish-class mistake. But because a student has a teacher coaxing him out of it, *Yo gusto las manzanas* goes by the wayside pretty fast for someone in a Spanish class.

But imagine if the way you learned Spanish was while making baskets somewhere, alongside other people who didn't speak it any better than you did, and where people who spoke Spanish natively didn't have enough interest in you to correct your speech. *Yo gusto las manzanas* could easily become common coin among your set, and in fact it probably would.

That's just how it was under Darius and the Achaemenids in Persia. The empire was routed by Alexander the Great in the 300s B.C. Once Persian reappears on paper under the Greek Seleucid reign, after a three-hundred-year blackout in writing, it is a new kind of language. This Persian, today known as Middle Persian, represented what had happened to the language under the influence of the construction workers and basket makers, so to speak. In terms of grammar it was, basically, Persian as it is now.

Case marking was now all but extinct, including the vowel-changing apparatus. The verb system represented a thorough housecleaning of the Latinoid thicket that it was in Old Persian. Plural marking was almost as simple as it is now. If the man at my apartment had come in not only out of the rain but out of the Seleucid Persia of two millennia before, then what he wrote down for me would have been pretty much as perplexing to me as the modern language was.

Meanwhile, however, other Iranian languages, not subject to so much assault and battery by adults, were on their way to being Pashtos rather than Persians. Over in the east of Iran, while Middle Persian was going about in a state of semi-undress compared to how decked out Old Persian had been, there were now-extinct languages like Sogdian and Bactrian rattling around with as many as six cases, the *big-boog* business, and the rest of the typical Indo-European dog-and-pony show.

And Pashto itself today is a Pashto. The Pashtun never ruled an empire and made legions of adults learn it. They are a tight bunch, cherishing their cultural unity and ancient lines of tribal descent, their lands isolated from the rest of the world by tall, craggy mountains. Pashto has been largely a language learned from the cradle. To the extent that outsiders have had to crack their teeth on it, there haven't been nearly so many that Pashtun children would start thinking of their "funny" rendition of it as a model to follow.

And today, of the forty or so other Iranian languages, some are more grammatically elaborate than others, but none are streamlined to the radical extent that Persian is. It isn't surprising that we hear so little about the other languages. The Kurds speak one, Kurdish, but we have only started to hear of them in the news since the Gulf War in 1991, and note that we hear all but nothing about their language, much less that it is related to Persian. There is a causal relationship between the obscurity of most Iranian languages and their complexity. If languages like Ossetic, Shugni, Balochi, and Tati were better known beyond where they are spoken, they would possibly owe their fame to having been imposed amidst empire upon adults—which would have sanded them down into a Persian-style *Bauplan*.

Modern Persian can be seen as either streamlined or stunted in comparison to Old Persian—but whatever it is, it does not represent the normal development of an Indo-Iranian language. Pashto is normal; Persian is a departure.

And not in a fashion that is uniquely Persian—there are many languages in the world that have gone through the same process. You're reading in one of them right now.

OUR MAGNIFICENT BATTERED TONGUE

English is one of about a dozen Germanic languages, the others including German, Swedish, Norwegian, Danish, Dutch, and Icelandic. Among them, English is the oddly "easy" one as grammatical complexity goes, very much "Germanic, Jr." Anything that challenges people learning Germanic languages is likely lost in only one of them: this one.

It's the only Germanic language in Europe without gender*— as well as the only Indo-European language in Europe without gender in any dialect. To us, *hither* and *thither* are joke words; in

---

* Except Afrikaans, spoken in South Africa, which lost gender because it was born amidst unusual conditions, as English was; Afrikaans is "Dutch, Jr." However, it is less "Junior" overall, in terms of Germanic complexity, than English is.

other Germanic languages, to distinguish between *Sit here* and *Come hither* is living language, as in German's *Komm her* rather than *hier*.

Or, what part of speech is *gone* in *She is gone*? Call it an adjective—and explain why you can't say *a gone dog* as you can say *a brown dog*. *She is gone* is English's wan gesture toward something robust in its Germanic relatives, in which a whole group of verbs take *be* instead of *have* in the past, because they describe something that is more how you are than what you did. To be gone is just that, to *be* gone. Sure, it is also technically to "have" exerted the action of leaving, but we think more readily of the result of the leaving, that one is in the state of *being* gone. Thus just as French has *Il est allé*, "He is gone," German has *Er ist gegangen*. All of the other Germanic languages have the equivalent, or almost all (what's up with you, Swedish?). English crudely forces *have* on every verb, and while Swedish does, too, that's just one coarseness, as if it happened not to learn to put a napkin in its lap but still went about in double-breasted suits and cultivated orchids. English, in comparison, just-the-facts-ma'am across the board, is Cro-Magnon.

Another one: in *forgive, forgo*, and *forbear*, what does *for-* mean? Or *with-* in *withstand* and *withhold*? In both cases, nothing, really—and *for-* and *with-* only occur in a few verbs. But those prefixes have live meaning in most other Germanic languages. In German, the *for-* equivalent *ver-* is a still handy way to make a word into a verb: in Pennsylvania, German speakers awkwardly termed the "Pennsylvania Dutch" say *verbotscht* for *all messed up*.

English was once normal, with *for-* lending a note of intensification: *bœrnan* was just *burn* while *forbœrnan* meant to utterly burn up. Old English, with its *hithers*, lots of verbs taking *be* in the past, its four cases, and so much else, was as busy in all ways as German and the other Germanic languages are now. Or as Pashto is. But after a while, things changed.

English, like Persian, was stunted by too many adults learning it for an extended period of time. In this case it was the

Scandinavian Vikings who invaded, starting in the eighth century A.D., and stayed on to marry local women and knit themselves into English society. As new waves of Vikings kept blowing in over generations, children grew up hearing as much "funny" English as native: that is, without gender, using *here* instead of *hither*, chucking the difference between *has seen* and *is departed*, and so on. Scribes kept writing Old English more or less as if this wasn't happening, but then, just as Alexander's invasion had interrupted Persian writing, the Norman Conquest put written English on pause.

For two centuries, the written language of England was French, and when English started being used on paper again, it was "Middle" in the same way as Persian when it came back to light—slimmed down and more user-friendly. Here was the language as it had been rendered by Viking foreigners. If English had been Ronald Reagan in the old movie *King's Row*, it would have woken up and asked, "Where's the rest of me?"*

Today, therefore, English is the "Persian" while the "Pashto" is less German than Icelandic, which retains three genders and four cases and remains a "real" Indo-European language in the style of Latin, Greek, Russian, and Sanskrit. Importantly, it's not that Icelandic is odd in staying so complicated—it's English that is odd in being so much less so.

HOW DO LANGUAGES GET NORMAL?

Thinking of languages as what they are in the immediate present, people seem to think of them as akin to clocks: integrated mechanisms serving to convey information. However, in a his-

---

* Despite my sounding that film buff note, the truth is that for me as a member of the generation who grew up overdosing on Looney Tunes on Saturday morning and local afternoon TV, the "Where's the rest of me?" line is much more immediately associated with Daffy Duck using it in *Duck Amuck* after Bugs Bunny erases his body.

torical perspective, languages are like kudzu. They grow hungrily, ceaselessly, and rampantly into available space, here sprouting multiple plural markers, there conjugating verbs differently according to whether they are about doing something to something (like throwing) or just about experiencing something (like falling).

The only thing that stops kudzu is some disturbance such as a pesticide. In the same way, the natural state of a language unless interrupted by foreign adults trying to learn it is ingrown, marking all kinds of distinctions that a language could do perfectly well without. Languages are like this not because such things are necessary to communication—in America we seem to get a fair amount done without having a dozen different plural markers. Languages are like this because they can't help it any more than kudzu can help growing—and babies can learn them regardless.

"The Girl Can't Help It," as the song and movie title put it in the fifties—and languages are similarly unable to not be ingrown. This is because speaking is, first, largely subconscious and, second, rapid. Below the level of consciousness and going by too quickly to think much about, speaking is ripe for habit-forming, for mission creep. Once something gets started, it has a way of hanging around and settling in—even when the language was doing just fine without it.

For example, how does a language end up with gender marking as in Spanish *la mesa blanca* for *the white table*? Clearly, no one decided one afternoon, "We hereby shall divide words into masculine and feminine groups rather randomly, and mark the masculine ones with an -*o* suffix and the feminine ones with an -*a* suffix."

As it happens, we can't know *precisely* how it happened in Spanish, because its earliest form preserved in writing, Latin, already has the gender markers, and even Latin's ancestor, the Proto-Indo-European that we can reconstruct, already had them. However, elsewhere in the world there are languages at an earlier stage in the development of gender that show us how such things can start. Chinese is one of them.

In Mandarin Chinese, when indicating a number of something, one uses a little word between the number and the noun depending on what kind of object it is. There are dozens of these little words, such as:

sān **zhī** māo "three cats" (for animals)
sān **tiáo** hé "three rivers" (for skinny things)
sān **zhāng** chuáng "three beds" (for flat things)
sān **ge** rén "three people" (for people [and other things])

They are called "classifiers," and while they don't at first bring to mind the way Spanish makes *gato*, "cat," a boy and *cama*, "bed," a girl with different suffixes, they are actually variations on that theme.

The closest equivalent to classifiers in English is when one says *three heads of cattle*, where we specify that the cattle come in "heads" when we could just as well say *three cattle* and would never say *three skinny things of river*. One might imagine an alternate universe where we did, and also said *three flatties of bed*. That alternate universe, as it were, exists—except in it, we're Chinese.

It's how Chinese got a battery of classifiers. The *zhī* for animals in Chinese, as in *sān zhī māo*, "three cats," started as a word for, roughly, "unit," and was used with animals just as *head* is in English for cattle. However, while in English the practice has remained a marginal construction used only in animal husbandry, there's no reason people speaking a language would *have* to stop there once something like that started. They might, and English speakers did. But they might not, and Mandarin speakers didn't. Mandarin started yoking other nouns into counting other types of things.

Languages drift into anality about different things. None are anal about everything possible; all focus on some things over others. English distinguishes *the* cat I bought in 1997 from *a* dog I wish I could buy but can't put in the commitment to walk several times a day. Mandarin has no articles and leaves that little nuance largely to context. It didn't happen to take on the article fetish that European languages tend to have, but instead took the *head of cattle*-type construction and ran with it.

The running with it in question meant that *tiáo*, which started out meaning "branch," was dragged into use with numbers applied to other skinny things, like rivers, roads, ropes, and tails. Meanwhile, *zhāng* took over to specify flat things, like beds and tables. Other nouns were treated the same way.

The written history of Chinese shows how classifiers entered the language as a gradual process. In Old Chinese, classifiers were used only optionally as a decorative form of expression, and there were only so many of them. It was still a language, like English, where you could just say *three cats* if you wanted to. But as Old Chinese became modern Mandarin, what began as a precious verbal flounce became a hard-and-fast rule—*all* nouns with numbers had to take a classifier of some kind. In Mandarin, when there's number, there's gender marking—i.e., nouns are divided into classes—just like in Spanish.

Then, languages of the world show us two further steps along the way to *la mesa blanca*.

First is what happens to classifiers in Cantonese. Mandarin is only one of several Chinese languages. Note that I write "languages" instead of "dialects" as it is often put regarding Mandarin versus Cantonese, or Taiwanese or Shanghainese. That's because these "dialects" are actually as different as French and Spanish and Italian. Different, but based on the same plan. Such that Cantonese has classifiers, too—but has gone beyond using them only with numbers.

Cantonese classifiers have, like kudzu, sprawled from number friends into being just articles of a sort. You use them even without numbers, just to specify what category something belongs to when you're pointing it out.

Broadway lyricist Fred Ebb said in the *Chicago* song "Mr. Cellophane," "Suppose you was a little cat / Residin' in somebody's flat . . ." But think about it—he wasn't referring to a cat that was especially small in stature. He was expressively pegging house-cats as being, in general, rather small, even if they are the fatter sorts. They only get so big—to summon the essence of cat-ness in that lyric, Ebb sweetly pegged them as little. As we might do with other things, in saying *That little kid*, for example, or, more to the point, *I saw a little mouse*—why do we say *little* when, after all, no mice are the size of cows?

The use of classifiers in Cantonese stems from what begins as this kind of expressive usage, such as of *little*, then takes it and runs with it, extending it to other adjectives English doesn't treat that way.

To wrap your head around how this makes sense, start with *a little mouse*, in the sense of *li'l*, not "of small size." And now try something equally unnecessary but charmingly expressive: *a flat ol' table*. Or *a skinny li'l pen*. Or a *cutey bubble of a button*. Now imagine that you were as much in the habit of saying things like that as you are of saying things like *little mouse*. Why, after all, is littleness so privileged as something to fetishize when you describe things, when there are so many other aspects of what things are like?

Note that regularly saying *a flat ol' table* and *a skinny li'l pen* hardly seems to strain the bounds of normal humanity; it's just that *we* don't do it. And add this: the father language Old Chinese used the classifiers with numbers, and so the Cantonese situation developed from the Mandarin-type one. Imagine, then, how much easier it would be to start saying *a flatty of a table* if at an earlier stage in the language speakers were already used to saying *three flatties of tables, five flatties of tables*.

And if you get that, you get how a habit formed in Cantonese that led to things like:

> **jēung** tói "a table" (a flatty of a table)
> **fūk** wá "a painting" (a flat-against-the-wall-y of a painting)
> **jī** bāt "a pen" (a skinny of a pen)
> **lāp** láu "a button" (a round little thingy of a button)
> **ga** chē "a car" (a gets-you-there of a car)

Then, we see one more step along the way to *la mesa blanca*, in that Papua New Guinea language Nasioi that has a hundred genders. Nasioi's gender is marked by classifiers as in Chinese, and they occur with numbers as in Mandarin. One of them, *ru'* (the ' is a catch in the throat like the one you utter before both syllables of *uh-oh*), marks bodies of water. In Nasioi, you use the classifier with not only the noun, but the words modifying it and even the number itself. Under this sentence, CL stands for classifier and PL for plural:

ntona-**ru'**	bee-**ru'**-pi	a-**ru'**-daang
lake-CL	three-CL-PL	this-CL-inland

"three lakes inland"

Here, what began as something like Mandarin's *sān tiáo hé*, "three rivers," is now as if in Mandarin one said *sān-tiáo hé-tiáo*. And then imagine people saying that quickly and without thinking over time, again and again, century after century, such that *tiáo* shortens into something like *-tá*, as we often utter *Let's go* as "tsgo." And then even later, say *-tá* erodes further into just *-a*. In a hypothetical Mandarin in 4000 A.D., *three rivers* could be *sān-a hé-a*. This is how languages start from something like Mandarin's *tiáo*, meaning, at first, "branch," and wind up at Spanish's meaningless little *-a* ending used on the adjective and the noun.

There was no reason for it, per se—it happens one step at a time, but is so transformative that a language can start like English, in which we just say *a white table*, and end up as a language that requires you to indicate what group a thing belongs in every time you mention it, and to do so with a suffix on not only the word itself but the other ones associated with it—*la mesa blanca*. This is how languages get complicated—and they always do.

From the point of view of English, it's natural to ask, "Why is Archi so complicated?" Technically, however, that's like asking "Why did they make that movie in color?" Just as the right question would be "Why did they make that movie in black-and-white?," the proper question about language is "Why is English so simple?"—or at least "Why isn't English as complicated as Archi?"

Anthropological linguist J. Peter Denny once illustrated this neatly with Kikuyu, a language of Kenya, which has a much richer array of words expressing closeness and distance than English. For one thing, the basic distinction between *here* and *there* applies to one's own perspective, with a third distinction referring to the perspective of the other person: so in Kikuyu there is *here*, *there*, and "how you see it." But that's just the beginning.

Within the *there* distinction as applied to oneself, there is a difference between a closer *there* and a farther *there*—approximately

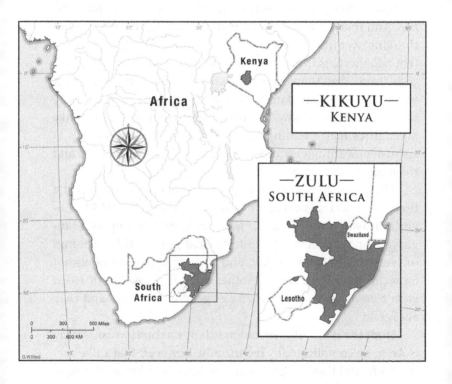

what you might in running speech label as "there, here" and "over there":

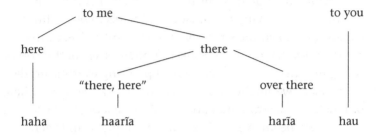

But then: all of these words have alternates that you use when referring to, basically, a wide open space rather than speaking within a home or other delineated space. So:

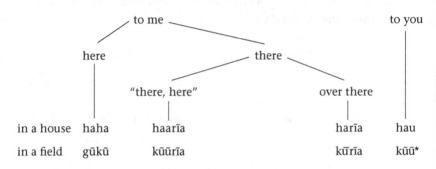

This means that while English just makes do with *here*, *there*, and then *over there* if we need it, Kikuyu has a four-way basic split, which itself splits again according to whether you are out in the open or "in here." Think: in Kikuyu there is a word that all by itself means "in here, there close to me."

Denny's idea was that Kikuyu is closer to nature itself than

---

* If one happens to know that a tilde signifies nasality, Kikuyu can look on the page as if it were a strangely ugly language to listen to, which it isn't. For the record, tildes in Kikuyu writing do not indicate nasality: ũ just means *o* and ĩ just means *e* (to get a tad more specific for those who care, they indicate the tense mid vowels "oh" and "ay" as opposed to the lax mid vowels "aw" and "eh").

English is, and that the actions of humankind decrease languages' naturalness. Denny ventured that English has less need for specific directional words because where it is typically spoken, there are so many man-made landmarks to place things in relation to—down the street, next to the post office. In the village societies that Kikuyu is spoken in there is less of this sort of thing, and therefore a richer array of pointing words is needed.

As such, we might assume that among the Eskimo, where for much of the year landmarks consist of igloos and little else, there would be an even richer array of pointers, and there are. In their Yupik language, in the basic sense there are twenty-two, with the same indoor/outdoor distinction Kikuyu has, plus *there* split into "up," "down," "in" and "out," and a vanilla one for good measure, and then different words for all of that when applying to your perspective rather than mine! Just within the realm of my perspective:

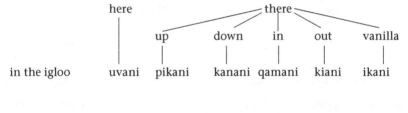

here		up	down	in	out	vanilla
in the igloo		uvani	pikani	kanani	qamani	kiani	ikani
out in the snow		maani	paani	unani	qamani	qaani	avani

Here is what happens when the man-made is especially thin on the ground, then.*

Denny's direct linkage of the number of placement words

---

* Looming here for many readers will be a certain question that is perhaps one of the four or five most often asked of linguists. My answer, in brief: (1) more words for *snow* than we have, although (2) much of the issue depends on what a "word" is, since in Eskimo languages, what English expresses as a sentence is often a single word, and (3) in any case, nowhere near "hundreds" or even dozens; more like, from what I have seen in my brief exposure to the subject and correspondence with its leading debate participants, seven.

to the modernity of a setting is, in itself, questionable. For one, countless languages are spoken in villages, on the steppe, and so on and yet have no splendid proliferations of placement words like Kikuyu and Yupik. In fact, most languages don't—one must smoke out such cases. Moreover, even when English was an Iron Age "tongue" spoken by small numbers of village folk, it only exceeded Modern English's tally by one, with ye olde *yonder* for "over there." More properly, Kikuyu and Yupik are languages that happened to develop a *here/there* fetish rather than one for classifiers or articles. That was the roll of the dice: humans could live, hypothetically, on a vast, flat plane out of a geometry textbook and come up with *here* and *there* as likely as they might come up with *right here, just over there by you*, and *way over there in here by him*.

The point is that only languages rarely learned by foreigners *could* retain a fetish taken as far as Kikuyu and Yupik took the one they happen to have drifted into. English didn't happen to develop a vast array of *here/there* words—it's not, in general, an Indo-European family obsession, much less a Germanic one. But if English had, the Vikings would likely have shorn away all but, roughly, *here* and *there*. The man-made intervention that makes the difference between Kikuyu and English is not the invention of skyscrapers, but blunted adult language-learning abilities.

These are "man-made" in the sense of being an outgrowth of transportation and military technology. The subjugation of massive populations, the ruling of them from afar, and the transportation of them across vast distances into central locations, where people speaking different languages had to learn a new one quickly, was unknown for most of *Homo sapiens'* history. Only when this sort of thing became possible was there any reason for a language to undergo the peculiar circumstance of being learned as much by adults as by children. Only then could there be languages like Modern English and Persian.

Before the emergence of empires and modern technology, presumably all languages were like Pashto and Yupik. Languages would have been spoken by small groups largely isolated from one another, and as such, there would rarely be a reason for anyone to learn a language past toddlerhood, and certainly not for large enough numbers of people to do so to affect how the language was passed down through generations. This would have meant that all languages were massively complex, ingrown affairs.

Thus, there is one language with a simple two-way distinction between *this here* and *that there*:

ini "this here"
itu "that there"

Another one is related to it as, roughly, Spanish is to English, but it has a six-way split, going far beyond just *ini* and *itu*:

ini "this here"
itu "that there"
maitu "that near him"
watu "that over there by him"
tatu "that up there"
nagha "that which we can hear but not see"

One of these languages has been used for centuries as a second-language lingua franca more than as a first. One of them is spoken by a mere 200,000 on some small islands. We can know that this latter is the one with the six-way split—because it would be all but impossible for the lingua franca to hold on to such a thing. Inevitably, all those busy adults have kept things down to just *ini* and *itu* in Indonesian, while a six-way split proliferates in the obscure Muna, spoken near the mega-island Sulawesi, best known to Westerners as the source of one of the coffees Starbucks sells.

There is one caveat to observe when thinking along those lines, however: Englishes and Persians have only arisen in antique, pre-Gutenbergian contexts where most people are illiterate and the printed page is of marginal import in society. In conditions like these, there was no omnipresent standard language set starkly against the "mistakes" that foreigners make. It allowed for change in how entire subsequent generations spoke a language. In our ultramodern condition, with widespread literacy, compulsory education, and omnipresent broadcast media, a language's standard version can survive as a model for speech regardless of how first-generation immigrants speak it.

Thus Russian is spoken as a second language across the former Soviet empire but remains the awesomely complex thing that all Slavic languages are. This is because Russian has been imposed mostly through education, and during a time when print, and later broadcast media, were ubiquitous. If Russian had spread across the same space a thousand years ago, or if massive populations from far eastward had been imported into Moscow or Kiev then, Russian today would likely be a weirdly user-friendly Slavic language with just one case left and two genders max, if any.

THE NORMALITY OF ABNORMALITY: MOROCCO AND HAITI

The world is bedecked neither with six thousand languages like English and Persian nor with six thousand languages like Pashto and Archi, but with six thousand languages occupying a range bounded by those extremes. There are, overall, a lot more Archis than Persians, as we would expect given that the vast majority of languages are little known and little learned beyond their small group. Yet quite a few languages have undergone the Persian conversion to assorted extents: an interruption in their histories that has sheared away a lot of the undergrowth that piles up in a language over thousands of years.

Arabic began as a language spoken mostly by bands of nomads in Arabia, little known beyond its confines. But when Mohammed brought speakers of this language together under a new Islamic empire in A.D. 630, Arabic met the world. Modern Standard Arabic is based on that nomad language, or more precisely its rendition as the Classical Arabic of the Koran, and is carefully preserved as it was when written a millennium-and-a-half ago. That Arabic is a Pashto, deeply specified in countless ways, often making it difficult for any but the most devoted students to get far beyond learning to read and write the script.

However, the Arabic varieties spoken where Islam was imported in subsequent centuries—of which today there are about a dozen from a "lumping" rather than "splitting" perspective—are quite different. They are, in fact, different languages from the standard and from one another, despite their designation as "dialects" because of the cultural and religious unity of the Arab world. Moroccan Arabic, for example, is to Modern Standard Arabic as French is to Latin.

This is partly because these colloquial varieties have functioned as spoken languages, rarely used in writing (although this is changing for some varieties today, such as Egyptian Arabic). Spoken language changes eternally, especially when there is no written version frozen on view as "the real thing," exerting a braking effect on departures from that. To a Moroccan, the Arabic of daily life is something in the mouth and almost never seen on the page. It has its own life apart from the standard.

But just as much of the difference is because Arabic, in its spread, was imposed on adults who already spoke other languages. The Arabic dialects that they created were not as shorn of bric-a-brac as English and Persian were. Arabic was imposed gradually, upon people still living in their native lands. There was time, over generations, for them to master more of the hard stuff than abruptly transplanted Vikings in England or laborers in Persia could. The local Arabics, then, remain robustly elaborate languages compared to their Classical ancestor, by no means seeming "easy" to the outsider. However, their elaboration is distinctly less robust than the standard's, to an extent inconceivable as mere accident.

Learn Arabic in a classroom, for example, and you have to master suffixes that mark not only case, but the difference between *the* and *a*:

bayt-u	the house	bayt-un	a house
bayt-a	the house (object)	bayt-an	a house (object)
bayt-i	of the house	bayt-in	of a house

But no need to worry about that in Moroccan Arabic or any other local kind, except in scattered shards.

Or, Standard Arabic verb conjugation is highly specified, or ingrown in our sense, in distinguishing not just person and number, but masculine from feminine, plus even a plural that refers to just two in addition to a more typical one meaning two or more. Here is just the second- and third-person plural endings for the past—where in Moroccan, the male-female and "just-two" issues are long gone, and things are the way we think of as normal (because Modern English is as "unnatural" as Moroccan Arabic!):

Standard		**Moroccan**	
you two wrote	katabtumā		
those two guys wrote	katabā		
those two gals wrote	katabatā		
you many guys wrote	katabtum	you people wrote	ktəbtu
you many gals wrote	katabtunna		
those many guys wrote	katabū	they wrote	kətbu
those many gals wrote	katabna		

In Morocco, Arabic was imposed upon Berbers speaking languages of their own (those languages were called Berber, for the record), as well as on 150,000 slaves brought from below the Sahara. It is hardly surprising that their rendition of Arabic was more meat-and-potatoes than the Classical one, and in fact it would be surprising if it had not been.

Slaves, as a matter of fact, were often in a position to take the streamlining process even *further* than what happened to English and Persian. In a plantation colony like Haiti, for example, slaves from west Africa speaking several different languages were transported to the island. Here was a situation where, first, there were massive numbers of people who needed to learn French very fast. On top of this, however, unlike in England, where the Vikings married local women, in Haiti slaves interacted with native French speakers only rarely. A typical sugar plantation had hundreds of slaves and just a few whites overseeing the operation.

One can imagine that in a situation like this, it would be hard to pick up much French beyond isolated words, and the reality was not far from that. The linguistic result in Haiti was not really French at all, but a new language based on French words, filled out into something that was one part French grammar, one part grammar from west African languages, and one part novelty.

The outcome of this process was very much a "real" language—we will return to its kind in Chapter Five (preview: this is what a *creole language* is). However, it was based on a vast abbreviation of the ingrown qualities of French. Here is a sentence in French and Haitian:

> French: Ils n'ont pas de ressources qui puissent leur permettre
> de résister.
> Haitian: Yo pa gen resous ki pou pèmèt yo reziste.
> "They don't have the resources to allow them to resist."

In French, *ont* is the third-person-plural form of *avoir*, "have," while in Haitian the *have* verb *gen* is the same with all persons and numbers. French renders *they* as *ils* and *them* as *leur*—Haitian renders both as *yo*. *Puissent* is in the subjunctive, French's hypothetical mood that bedevils us English speakers, encoding that the people don't have the resources that *could* allow them to resist. Haitian is no more dedicated than English is to marking hypotheticality as obsessively as French does. French has *de ressources*, with that subtle usage of *de*, "of," that is also tough for foreigners. Let us salute the creators of Haitian for letting that go completely.

In this and many other ways (such as that there is no gender of the *le soleil/la lune* variety), Haitian has eliminated most of what makes French challenging to acquire beyond childhood. This is for the simple reason that the people who created it were past childhood and talking almost only to one another. This doesn't make Haitian "not a language." For one thing, as we have already seen and will see more of in Chapter Three, grammar is more than endings. Besides, the massive degree of complexity that a language winds up clotted with if left alone is hopelessly unnecessary. No one *needs* to distinguish that resistance that has yet to happen is—golly!—hypothetical, which is what subjunctive marking does. This, like the development of classifiers and gender suffixes, is the product of blind, stepwise changes over vast periods of time, as imperceptible to individual speakers within their short lives as natural selection is in the natural world.

Yet because this mad, creeping accretion is inevitable, a language with little of it can only emerge from artificial conditions, of a kind that did not exist during most of the time that humans were speaking. Left to its own devices over millennia, no language has a grammar like Haitian Creole's. There'd be no way for it to. Uninterrupted, language is massively and irrepressibly ingrown.

THE PERSIAN CONVERSION AS A KEY TO THE PAST: THE KEO PUZZLE

Language is so irrepressibly ingrown that comparative ingrownness can give clues to historical events otherwise dimly recorded, if at all. Years ago I was skimming a linguistics article about the language family called Austronesian. It's enormous, a good one thousand languages stretching from the Philippines through the islands of Indonesia and then all the way eastwards across the coastline of New Guinea and on out into the South Seas, only stopping at Rapa Nui (Easter Island). In my mind, Indo-European languages are snow, Semitic languages like Arabic and Hebrew are sand, and Austronesian languages are coconuts.

In passing, my eye caught a word: *analytic*. At first I kept reading, but that word hovered between my conscious and subconscious and wouldn't let go. *Analytic*. Finally I went back to find the passage.

Analytic, in linguistic jargon, is an unfortunately opaque term that refers, simply, to a language having no prefixes or suffixes. Many don't or barely do; they're especially common in Africa and East and Southeast Asia. Chinese, then, is analytic. Here's a Mandarin sentence:

Tā chàng	de	hǎo	tīng
he sings	"-ly"	nice	hear

"He sings beautifully."

There's no equivalent to English's -*s* for the third person singular, and there is a separate word *de* to indicate the adverbial instead of a suffix like -*ly*.

English is not analytic, nor, obviously, is Pashto or Archi. Nor—and this was what grabbed me—are Austronesian languages. Just as in English, a typical sentence has at least one prefix or suffix hanging around. Tagalog in the Philippines has, in this sentence, a prefix marking the past. Actually, it's one of several past prefixes depending on whether . . . actually, never mind; Tagalog, let's just say, is complicated in a very typical way:

Na-kita	mo	siya	kahapon.
saw	you	him	yesterday

"You saw him yesterday."

Quite often, Austronesian languages have a lot more prefixes or suffixes than this. Here is a sentence of Tukang Besi, spoken on Sulawesi, not far from that Muna language I mentioned:

No-	**to- pa-**	ala-	**mo**	na iai-su	te kau.

he, really-was-made-fetch-"-ed"   younger sibling-my   wood
"My younger sibling was made to fetch some wood."

This is what Austronesian languages are like, one language after another, across a huge expanse of the planet. Austronesian is, like Indo-European, a family of languages, and members of families are, after all, similar. And so: analytic? An Austronesian language? It just doesn't make sense. "Analytic Austronesian language" written in passing reads as if a newspaper article read:

Yesterday at Sea World, one of the walruses spoke to its
trainer, informing her that one of the turnstiles at the
entrance to the tank stadium was stuck. After repairing the
turnstile, the maintenance staff, in view of the fact that such
malfunctions have been especially common with turnstiles
from the park's main equipment supplier of late, suggested
exploring other bidders in the future. The decision process
will likely be protracted . . .

"But *wait*, what about . . . !!" we would think. "Analytic Austronesian," just tossed off in the same way, elicited the same response in me.

It turned out that these analytic Austronesian languages are spoken on the little island of Flores, which is one of many in the string of islands between Bali and Timor. Sulawesi is just northwards and is flecked with prefix-heavy languages, like Tukang Besi. And in the nearby islands, languages are similarly decked out in prefixes and/or suffixes. On little Leti, the language has suffixes to indicate that you heard something rather

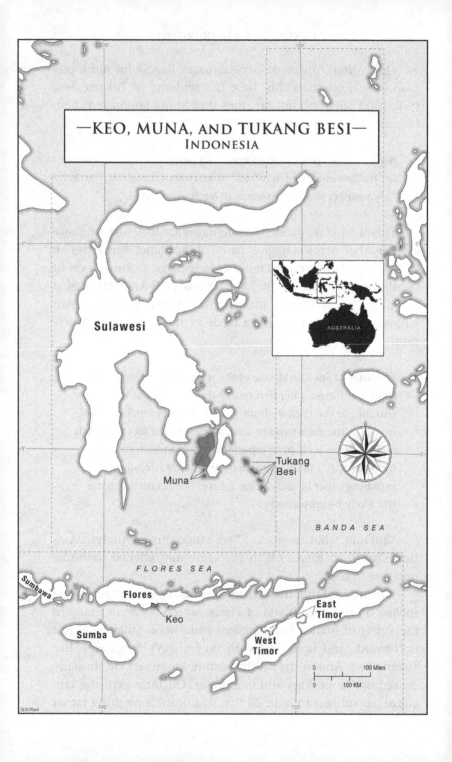

—KEO, MUNA, AND TUKANG BESI—
INDONESIA

Sulawesi

AUSTRALIA

Tukang
Besi

Muna

BANDA SEA

FLORES SEA

Sumbawa

Flores

Keo

East
Timor

Sumba

West
Timor

100 Miles

100 KM

G.W.Ward

than saw it, like Archi, and another one that specifies that what you're saying *isn't* subjunctive (really!):

Ra-	mtïĕtan-**nòr- e**	kadèr-**o**.
they-sit-	with-"I heard it"	chair-"for real"

"They use a chair to sit on."

In light of which a Flores language like Keo is a talking walrus. Here's a Keo sentence. No prefixes, no suffixes. Suddenly an Austronesian language is like Chinese.

Ghonggé	ndé,	dima	'imu	mélé	ka.
grope	that	arm	her	stuck	"-ed"

'uru	né'é	kara	subho.
because	have	bracelet	shell bracelet

"When she was groping in the hole, her arm got stuck because she had a shell bracelet."

Keo is one of a half dozen deeply obscure languages on Flores that are like this. Ngadha is also Mandarinesque in how things are put:

Maë	vela	cata.
not	kill	person

"You shouldn't kill anyone."

Another one is called Ende, so telegraphic that you have to fill in with context that this sentence means that the dog "exists to her" rather than that she is, herself, canine:

Kai	rhatu	rako.
she	exist	dog

"She has a dog."

If languages are naturally ingrown, and if the way that Austronesian languages are ingrown is that they have prefixes and suffixes, then for these few languages to not have any prefixes and suffixes is a queer, queer business. Austronesian languages were all born from a grandfather language that had prefixes and suffixes, and when that language branched out into a thousand new ones, they all carried that family trait along—except this little gang on Flores.

Where'd the prefixes and suffixes go? Was it that one day a generation of kids decided "This junk has got to go!" and stopped using the prefixes and suffixes their parents were using? Even imagining how such a thing would happen over several generations is impossible. One generation decides "Well, *re-*, *-s*, and *-en* are cool, but let's drop this *-ed* thing from now on," and then their kids for some reason decide "You know, isn't it time to drop this plural *-s*? And later we can talk about this damned *un-* . . . ," until finally the language was prefixless and suffixless. This just isn't the way languages or people work.

It'd be one thing if Flores had been, like Haiti, an island dedicated to plantation slavery, with adults speaking several languages thrown together to learn a new one. But Flores was never used in this way. It's just an island that some people live on—and have forever. No—it couldn't be quite that simple, because if it were, then the languages of Flores would be like their relatives Tukang Besi and Leti and the hundreds of others spoken around them.

The fact that they aren't leads to a particular conclusion. At some point, adults must have come to Flores and learned the local languages only partially and left them less ingrown than Austronesian languages are under normal conditions. That is, something as seemingly unremarkable as not having prefixes and suffixes shows us that in the past, the languages of Flores underwent a Persian conversion.

To test whether this way of approaching the case is correct, though, we need other evidence. Written history will be of little help, however—Flores societies were oral ones until the Western encounter starting in the 1500s. Even after that, Flores was just one island among quite a few, and Dutch and Portuguese observers had little interest in chronicling population movements between it and other islands. Archaeology, meanwhile, is in its infancy on Flores. As such, the only other place to look would be the languages themselves. If Flores languages were picked up by adults at some point, then what evidence might remain other than the "haircut" effect of the loss of the prefixes and suffixes?

Well, one thing we would expect if a language was overrun by people who grew up with another one is that these people would pepper their rendition of the Flores language with a lot of words of their own. Yiddish-speaking Jews in America retained words like *schlemiel*, *meshugenah*, and *nebbish* in their English, for example. More to the point, that process can go much further—exhibit A was the Vikings in England. Making do with their crummy Old English, they plugged so many of their Old Norse words into it that we can barely get through a sentence without them: *get*, *they*, *wrong*, *take*, *anger*, *bag*, *low*, *club*, *knife* (funny what kind of people that list makes the Vikings look like, but from reports it doesn't seem far off).

What, then, are the vocabularies of the Flores languages like? As it turns out, quite bizarre. This is clear when we see how things look when *not* bizarre.

Austronesian speakers came to the area where Flores is about thirty-five hundred years ago, quickly covering the various islands. This means that the languages spoken in this region today, perched on their separate islands and morphing along as languages always do, have been developing separately for over three thousand years. The result of that kind of separation is that equivalent words in the languages will become different from one another—similar, but different, variations on a theme, just like French's *main*, Spanish's *mano*, and Portuguese's *mão* after roughly two thousand years of separation from the Latin original, *manus*.

Then, in other cases, a language may have replaced its

equivalent to a word with another one. The word *bird* in English, for example, "should" be *fowl*, descended from the same Proto-Germanic word that has become *Vogel* in German and Dutch, *fågel* in Swedish, *fugl* in Danish, and *foigel* in Yiddish. And in Old English, the word was indeed *fugol*. But for some reason English took a word that initially meant "little bird" (or maybe "born creature"*) and made it the default word, relegating *fowl* to a more specialized meaning (what, really, is a fowl?). That leaves a hair out of place for English in a comparative list of Germanic languages' vocabularies.

We can see both of these processes in languages of Flores and the surrounding area. Let's go with our friend Tukang Besi and four languages spoken on other islands in the area.† The words in italics are the "bird" cases, the ones that aren't developments of the same root as the one Tukang Besi uses.

Come, for example, is *mai* in Tukang Besi, *maa* in Kei, *ma* in Yamdena, and *'a-ma* in Dobel—all obviously divergences from the same root but distinct—while Nusa Laut and Asilulu have taken on different words entirely. And even when the words are divergences from the same root, often we're talking serious divergence. *Be thirsty* in Tukang Besi is *moro'u*, and comes out fairly similarly as *ma'raw-ni* in Dobel (if you ignore that -*ni* part that drifted in at some point). But in Nusa Laut we have to work to see the relationship of *moro'u* to *amalael*: it has taken on

---

* For those interested in some heavy-duty etymology, I recommend Anatoly Liberman's *An Analytic Dictionary of English Etymology* (Minneapolis: University of Minnesota Press, 2008), which clears the brush away from a collection of long-standing etymologies, one of them being the standard "birdie" account of the origin of *bird*.

† Tukang Besi, with its two words, seems such an odd name for a language, I know—it looks like someone's name. And it is, in a way: it means *"iron worker"* in Indonesian, the lingua franca of the area. If you must have a more conventional sounding name for it, one is Wakatobi.

	Tukang Besi	Nusa Laut	Asil-ulu	Kei	Yam-dena	Dobel
come	mai	*tawae*	*kawae*	maa	ma	'a-ma
dead	mate	mataen	matate	maat	mat	'a-kʷoy
fish	ika	yano	íane	*vuut*	ian	si'a
fowl	manu	manuo	manu	manut	manik	*toru*
liver	ate	ata-	*wélua*	yatan	ati	sata
pig	wawu	hahul	hahu	vaav	babi	ɸaɸi
rain	usa-	*kialo*	úlane	*doot*	udan	kʷusan
stone	watu	hatul	hatu	vaat	bati	ɸatu
sugar cane	towu	tohul	tehu	tev	tefu	kʷuŋar
be thirsty	moro'u	amalael	*letasele*	nebroo	*manges*	ma'raw-ni
tree	hu'u	*aiwonyo*	úwene	*vuak*	*katutun*	'ay
worm	ulo	*retal*	*salálene*	uar	ule	kʷaytuba

an initial *a* and a final *l*, the vowels have changed, and *moro'u*'s *r* has gone to *l* (itself not surprising; think of Chinese and Japanese speakers who initially confuse them in English). And we won't even get into what turned *moro'u* into Kei's *nebroo*; suffice it to say that this is all typical of what happens when related languages have been morphing along by themselves for thousands of years.

Which brings us to the *bizarrerie*: look at Tukang Besi compared to four of the Flores languages after three thousand years plus:

	T. Besi	**Ende**	**Ngada**	**Rongga**	**Keo**
come	mai	mai	mai	mai	ma'i
dead	mate	mata	mata	mata	mata
fish	ika	ika	ika	ika	'ika
fowl	manu	manu	manu	manu	manu
liver	ate	ate	ate	até	'até
pig	wawu	wawi	wawi	wawi	wawi
rain	usa-	ura	uza	nura	'ura
stone	watu	watu	vatu	watu	watu
sugar cane	towu	tëwu	təvu	tewu	tewo
be thirsty	moro'u	moa	moa	mara	moa
tree	hu'u	puu	pu'u	pu'u	pu'u

The words have often barely diverged if at all, and there are no "birds." It's so tidy it's aesthetically pleasing*—but also too peculiar to be an accident.

We can see how truly weird this congruence is via comparing the same words in two languages elsewhere in the world. Let's bring back good old Kikuyu and compare it with its relative Zulu. Both are in the Bantu group, whose best-known member is Swahili: their grammars are as similar as French's is to Spanish's. They have been separated for probably *less* than three thousand years—and yet the relationship between the words is the faint kind you can glean between your own face and that in a photograph of a great-great-grandparent. Time has passed.

---

* Of course the entire vocabularies of these languages do not line up this perfectly. Plenty of Flores languages' words are as different from Tukang Besi equivalents as Portuguese's *mão* is from Latin *manus*, and Flores languages have their "bird" words as well compared to Tukang Besi. The point is, however, that such a large proportion of the vocabulary does match up like this, which is not remotely the case between Tukang Besi and other languages of the region. With these other languages, it would typically be difficult to present a list of matchups even this brief.

	Kikuyu	**Zulu**
come	ŭka	za
dead	kua	fa
fish	tega	inhlanzi
fowl	ngŭkŭ	inkuku
liver	ini	isibindi
pig	ngŭrŭe	ingulube
rain	mbura	imvula
stone	ihiga	itshe
sugar cane	kigwa	umoba
be thirsty	nyota	ukoma
tree	mŭtĭ	umuthi

Why would words just in Tukang Besi and a few languages of Flores sit frozen or virtually so for thirty-five hundred years? It simply doesn't follow that the vocabularies would match up that perfectly—or, it only follows if the languages have *not* been separate for thirty-five hundred years.

That is, suppose Tukang Besi words were brought into the Flores languages a lot more recently than thirty-five hundred years ago?

Here is where the absence of prefixes and suffixes becomes key. There are two things odd about Keo, Ngadha, and crew: (1) nakedness and (2) vocabularies strangely close to that of a language spoken on another island. As it happens, those two things are easy to bring together under a single explanation.

Presumably, the Flores languages were at first as ingrown as Tukang Besi and other Austronesian languages of the area. Tukang Besi–speaking adults would have come to Flores in significant numbers and stayed. They would have learned Flores languages as best as they could but never got very good at it. That would take care of the prefixes and suffixes. Meanwhile, spending as much or more time with one another than with

Floresians, they would speak the Floresian languages with a great deal of vocabulary from the homeland, just as the Vikings did in England.

New generations would hear as much of this kind of speech as the original language. There was no writing, schooling, printed matter, or broadcasts to allow the old language to keep its foot in the door. Language was what you heard, not what you read or saw written. And what the kids were growing up hearing was a prefixless and suffixless language full of Tukang Besi words. Pretty soon, you had languages like Keo.

The most plausible situation for such a thing would be if Tukang Besi speakers invaded Flores just as the Vikings did England—and as it happens, what shards of history we have of the relationship between Sulawesi and Flores show us that (1) there was a relationship and that (2) it involved Sulawesians migrating to Flores and staying there.

From the mid-seventeenth to the mid-eighteenth centuries, a Sulawesi kingdom *ruled* one-half of Flores, for one. Then, folklore among Flores groups includes tales of origin in Sulawesi. The absence of prefixes and suffixes in Flores puts us on a treasure hunt that leads us first to vocabulary relationships and then to folkloric material that alone might seem fictional but that in combination with the linguistic evidence confirms a sociohistorical relationship that is otherwise knowable only through the gauzy filter of legend.

Research on the relationship between Austronesian languages and the social history of Indonesia is still young, and details remain to be worked out about the relationship between Sulawesi and Flores. However, awareness of the ingrown essence of language can assist us in reconstructing things that happened ages ago to people who could not write about them.*

---

* What archaeology there has been, however, has unearthed remains of the "hobbit" people, likely a new species of human, *Homo floresiensis*. While those remains are at least thirteen thousand years old, folklore records similar people living on Flores as recently as a few centuries ago, with too much detail and explicit setting off from "spirits" and such not

BUT WHAT'S THE COMPLEXITY *"FOR"*???
THE KET MIRACLE

Even if we are aware that what is unusual is when a language is less complicated rather than when it is extremely complicated, a temptation always looms to attribute the complexity of language to some kind of utility. The idea that it is due to something as wan as drift or incremental habit formation sits awkwardly in the mind, especially for speakers of a moderately complex a language as English. Surely, we may think, all of that machinery in a language like Pashto must be *for* something. It couldn't just be buildup, like some ring in a bathtub.

The authors of a neat article on the topic, for example, nicely show that languages are more complex the more isolated their societies are—but then as the presentation winds down, they feel a need to figure out what the complexity is "for." Their guess is that when a language marks, say, the plural on articles, adjectives, and nouns (*las mesas blancas*) or when it has different conjugation patterns according to whether verbs are transitive or intransitive, this is a trait chosen by natural selection in the development of our species to assist children in learning languages, by being maximally explicit.

The problem here is that the actual ways that languages are complicated vastly overshoot anything that would be of any use to a child getting a grip on the system. To truly understand what

---

to be the real thing. For a while after this archaeological discovery was announced in 2003, I entertained an idea that the unusual nature of Flores's languages had something to do with these "hobbit" people, but in the end the idea doesn't go through. All recollections of them record that they lived apart from *Homo sapiens* and were processed as freakish. This would mean there would be no reason for them to learn *sapiens* languages to any significant extent—and even less reason for *sapiens* to start talking like the hobbits, which is what would have been required for the way the hobbits spoke to change the language entirely.

we are asking with a question like "Why are some languages so much more grammatically specified than others?" as the authors of this article phrase it, we must keep in mind what "grammar" really is in so very many languages in the world.

For example, to assess the idea that prefixes and suffixes— and by extension, the general ingrown quality of language uninterrupted—is an adaptational advantage designed to assist children in learning language, let's start with a little test. Here are two words in Italian:

vengo "I come"
vado "I go"

Now, just based on them, what part of those words would you say means "I"? Notice that this would hardly be a head-scratcher even if you didn't know a word of the language or a related one.

But let's try this. Here are two words in another language:

diksives "I come"
bɔɣatn "I go"

What part means "I"? Keep scratching.

Or, here is the same language's verb for "to extract, to free" with assorted parts indicating the pronouns, like -o in Italian (just to give you the answer since it was so hard to glean!). So what's I? Your first possible answer should keep in mind the third of these words. Or, how do you say just "to free," based on these three renditions?

dbatkuraq "I freed you."
kbatɔndaq "You freed me."
dbatɔndaχin "They freed me."

If it looks like there's just no way to figure it out, there barely is, from these five words. In fact, well into the 1980s even linguists hadn't figured out how to conjugate a simple verb in this language—partly because, really, there are no simple ones.

The language is called Ket and is spoken now by only a few hundred people in Siberia. It will soon no longer be spoken, it would appear, but when it was thriving, it was only ever spoken by a few thousand people at a time. As we would expect of such a language, it is very, very complicated—so much so that it strains belief that anyone actually speaks it.

For one thing, the answer to the first question about the pair of verbs is that both *di-* on the first one and *bɔ-* on the second one mean *I*. Ket has two whole sets of prefixes like this as pronouns— and one class of verbs takes one, while another takes the other, and you just have to know, for hundreds of verbs! It's the equivalent to conjugational classes like the *-er/-ir/-re* one in French, except that no endings like that tip you off as to which class a verb belongs to.

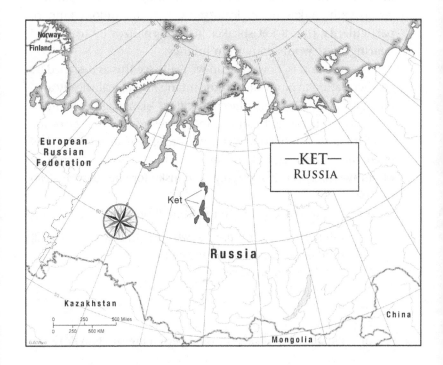

And it gets even worse: many verbs in Ket take two pronoun prefixes meaning the exact same thing. But then many don't. This divides verbs into subconjugations within the *di-/bɔ-* "conjugation." So *digdabatsaq* means "I go to the river," with both the *d* and *ba* meaning "I." Not "two I's," as in something like a cute way of getting a "we"; just "I." Kind of like if we said in English *I go to I the river.*

But then, the "subconjugations" can have meanings: a verb's meaning can change depending on how and even whether you double the pronoun. More specifically, ***d**igda**b**atsaq* means that I go to the river and come right back a little later. But if I use not two different *I*'s, but the same *I*-prefix twice, then that—***d**igda**d**daq*—is how to say I go to the river and stay for the season. And then, if I just use one prefix—i.e., what we think of as the "normal" thing to do—***d**igdaksaq* means that I go to the river and stay for some days or weeks. That these particular prefix options mean these very particular things with this particular *go* verb makes no logical "sense." It's a random kind of particularity that a Ket speaker just internalizes by using and hearing these words daily from infancy.

The question is, however: can we really see this as designed by Mother Nature to be an *aid* to those infants? More realistically analyzed, all of this is a magnificent accident—language as ingrown as it can be, because it can be, and therefore is. What favor are we doing little Junior cooing at him words like *dbatɔndaχin*, "they freed me"? Even said slowly and in the singsong cadence of Mommy-talk, this is like playing Stravinsky for your baby instead of Mozart.

There's a whole sentence in the word: it breaks down like this:

d-   third person (and not *they*; see what happens later in the word)
ba-   third person again (for no reason!!!)
t-   "-ing"ness (progressive)
ɔ-   in the past
n-   me
daχ- free
in   plural (which makes the third person prefixes into *they*)

And to answer the question as to what the root for *to free* is, it's *daq*, which comes out as *daχ* in *dbatɔndaχɨn* because *q* changes to *χ* before certain suffixes, like *f* becomes *v* before the plural marker in English words like *knives* and *lives*. Ket has a lot more of that kind of thing than English does, too—more fun for baby! (At least he gets to trill his uvula.)

If Ket were designed with children in mind in any way, it would be less a leg up than a torture chamber. It has, on top of all of the rest, crazy gender as we expect of a "real" language: trees are male, thumbs are female—but most body parts are neuter! Meanings of words are expressed partly with tone like in Chinese: *s'ul'* can mean "cradle hook,"* "blood," or "sled" depending on how you say it. And wouldn't you know it has eleven cases, including one to mark that something is going through another thing (!).

The only thing about this language that seems remotely infant-friendly is the unprecedentedly compact words for *I eat it* and *He eats it*: *dip* and *dup*. I can see a baby getting a kick out of that. But *digdabatsaq*? I'm sorry, but that's almost child *abuse*.

LANGUAGES ARE COMPLICATED BECAUSE they can be. They complicate as a natural result of millennia of habits developed by people using them quickly and unconsciously. Because babies can pick languages up despite the massive accretion of complexity this yields, languages stay complex—unless something intervenes, such as grown-ups learning them. Languages *are* like bathtub rings. For whatever it's worth, viewed under a microscope, bathtub rings are complex, teeming slices of biology. But that doesn't mean they serve a purpose.

Alison Wray and George Grace, in another paper on this issue, get it right. The languages of Early Man would have been

---

* I haven't the slightest idea.

Kets, which we adults would despair of learning—while children would pick them up without a thought:

> Our linguistically aware adult time-traveller would struggle
> to learn these languages, impeded by the proliferation of
> difficult sound combinations, wayward form-meaning
> pairings (perceived as irregularities), and the impenetrable
> semantic representations that are characteristic of languages
> used for esoteric communication. On the other hand, her
> intrepid two-year-old co-adventurer would achieve the task
> of acquisition with the natural aplomb of a human infant.

Many of the languages we are most familiar with are the result of the struggles adults faced with the task of that time-traveler.

It's why Mandarin, the Chinese variety most often learned by foreigners in China's history, has fewer tones and classifiers (and almost everything else) than Cantonese. It's why east Africa's lingua franca Swahili, unlike its relatives Kikuyu and Zulu, has *no* tones. It's why when I wrote this sentence, *sentence* had no gender and I didn't need to use a conjugational ending for *write*. It's why Keo and Ket differ so much more than in the final letter of their names.

Yet there's something that all languages, whether the products of that struggle or not, have in common. A language may be insistently particular about marking fine shades of meaning; a language may be breezily comfortable with leaving things to context. But in either case it is always, frankly, a mess.

For a sense of what I mean, let's go back to World War II.

CHAPTER TWO

LANGUAGE IS DISSHEVELED

It is not uncommon to hear about the Navajo code talkers, who served in the marines during the Second World War. The Japanese were so good at breaking U.S. codes that the top brass were receptive when Philip Johnston, who had grown up the son of missionaries on a Navajo reservation, suggested using the Navajo language as a code that no one on earth could crack.

Not even a Navajo: the code talkers did not simply speak their language, but devised a code within it. The word for *grenade* was the Navajo word for *potato*; *battleship* was *whale*, *dive bomber* was *chicken hawk*. There was also an alphabet key for spelling things out. *A* was the Navajo word for something that begins with *A* in English, *ant*: "wollachee" (*wóláchíí* in the actual orthography). *I* was the word for *intestine* (*ach'íí*), and *J* the one for *jackass*. A Navajo ABC book for kids could be interesting.

The code worked. The Japanese never cracked it—"a weird succession of guttural, nasal, tongue-twisting sounds," they later recalled—and the code talkers were crucial in the Iwo Jima victory. They also served in Korea and early in the Vietnam War. Yet truth to tell, Navajo would have presented almost as much of a hurdle to decoding even if the men had been talking *about* ants, intestines, and jackasses instead of using the words for them as code. This is in large part because of something about Navajo utterly normal—except that Navajo happens to be more normal than usual. It's a kind of normality that puts in a different light what we think of as normal—or more specifically, even proper—in English.

NAVAJO: WHERE EXCEPTIONS *ARE* THE RULE

Given that only a few dozen of the hundreds of languages spoken by Native Americans before the arrival of Europeans are being passed on to children today, it is always heartening to see the attention that Navajo gets in the media because of the code talkers. It would be easy for no one to know of a language spoken in a patch of an area in Arizona, New Mexico, Utah, and Colorado, just as barely anyone hears a thing about Navajo's neighbor and close relative Apache.

However, Navajo looks a lot different from underwater than it is portrayed in documentaries and on Web sites. We hear of Navajo as a "code," with the potatoes and chicken hawks and the "Roger Wilco–type" alphabet key. Even the official *Navajo Code Talkers' Dictionary*, declassified in 1968, lists the code words, the alphabet terms, and then countless words of just Navajo itself all as a piece, as if the code talkers were speaking English but plugging in Navajo words. In reality, most of their communication was in Navajo, period. They were using a language, a "tongue," an "idiom"—communicating at lightning speed and with little effort in not only an unfamiliar vocabulary, but also a grammatical system utterly alien to ours.

To linguists, in fact, Navajo is notorious for how unapproachable it is to the newcomer, beyond whatever words its speakers may have had to come up with for things like grenades and dive bombers. It is so superlatively forbidding that even linguists have trouble making sense of it. It pops up in linguists' conversations as an all-purpose example of a language that is an especially tough nut to crack—"It isn't Navajo, but I had to spend some time figuring out how it worked." The main go-to description of Navajo

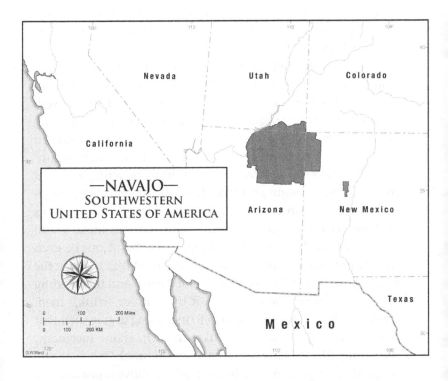

—NAVAJO—
SOUTHWESTERN
UNITED STATES OF AMERICA

grammar presents a system so fearsomely complex that it has to be approached almost like the Talmud, requiring slow, close-up study and always leaving questions. I remember running up against this book when I was a graduate student, trying to figure out one little thing about Navajo—it was like trying to make sense of electrical grid blueprints for the United Nations building.

Unsurprisingly, then, one of Johnston's arguments for using Navajo as a code was that it is so devilishly difficult that it's almost impossible to learn much of after childhood. In other words, Navajo is a Ket. Navajo may even, in a sense, *be* Ket. It has been proposed that Ket's ancestors were the source of the languages that later became Navajo and its kin when humans migrated from Asia to North America.

In the 1940s only about thirty outsiders could really speak Navajo, and this was a sign of what had helped make the language so difficult. Adults have only ever learned it rarely, nowhere near often enough for kids to hear foreigners speaking it as much as they hear their families doing so.

The difficulty that piles up as the result of this is partly, of course, "Archi"-tecture—kudzu-style overgrowth into tiny nooks and crannies. Here is a language where you use a special verb form when you mean something as specific as that something not only went on for a while, but went on for a while and then culminated in a pointed fashion. Romance languages distinguish the ongoing imperfect from the abrupt preterite, such that in French one is taught a sentence like "The students were (ongoingly) studying when the bell (suddenly) rang"—*Les étudiants étudiaent quand la cloche a sonné.* Navajo, too, can make a verb indicate either the ongoing or abrupt alone, but it can be even further ingrown. It can make a verb, in one stroke, indicate the whole scene of something going on for a while and then ending in a pointed way. The form *chin* of the verb for "stink," then, means "to have taken on a stench to increasing degree such that one is currently distinctly stinksome." Or, more succinctly, something like "to have acheived a state of 'stank.'"

And that "wind-up-and-then-bang!" narrative is just one of a great many in the language. We won't even get into the forms you use for describing a single occasion of stinking as singled out vividly from several others, or how you say that you are trying, for some reason, to smell bad. Yes, you *could* want to say that: remember that Pepé le Pew Looney Tune* where the cat decides she wants Pepé and locks herself in a Limburger cheese factory to make herself reek so that she can stand his odor? Well, in Navajo you could talk about that scene using a special verb form! Just once over the past fifty years I'll bet some kid actually has.

BUT AS THE WORLD'S LANGUAGES go, as we have learned, Archi-tecture is normal. The additional problem in Navajo is

---

* *Really Scent* (1959), in case you just must have a look.

that there is so very much that is plain arbitrary. You learn some bit of something and look for the rule for its use, only to find that for the most part there barely is one—if at all. It can seem like trying to grasp anything about Navajo is like trying to get a grip on a droplet of mercury. If you *could* pick Navajo up and you shook it, it would sound like a box full of Legos.

One thing rattling around in that box would be the verbs. Navajo is a language in which, as gorgeously counterintuitive as this is to imagine for speakers of almost any other language, there is no such thing as a regular verb. Let's take a perfectly ordinary verb, the one for "to move something rope-like."

Now, that in itself is weird from an English perspective but it's just Archi-tecture again, an ancient grammar growing in upon itself and marking unnecessarily fine shades. A verb for moving rope-like objects is the equivalent to Mandarin having little words used with long, skinny things. It's just that where Mandarin does it with particle words yoked to numbers, Navajo does it with verb forms about handling things (as opposed to with all verbs—even in Navajo there is no verb for "to stink like twine").*

What rattles is how this verb changes form from tense to tense and beyond. For our purposes, Navajo has five basic ones—present, past, future, repetitive, and subjunctive. Here are those five forms for *move a rope-like thing*:

---

* There are those who see things like this as meaning that speaking Navajo makes its speakers more sensitive to the shapes of things than we are. I am skeptical of that school of thought, as I devoted a chapter to in *Our Magnificent Bastard Tongue*. This aspect of Navajo is one of countless reasons why. For example, one study showed that Navajo-speaking children were more sensitive than white American ones to the shape of toys rather than their size or color. But then another one showed that in New York, white middle-class kids were even more sensitive to the shape of toys than Navajo kids had been shown to be, and also more than black ones from Harlem. The researcher concluded that the reason was likely that the white kids simply had more toys. Both the white and the black kids spoke English, and obviously white American English has no verbs meaning things like "to wield a rope-like object" that are unknown to black people. What made the difference was cultural experience, not grammar channeling the way the children think.

present	lé
past	lá
future	lééł
repetitive	lééh
subjunctive	lééł

For the record, the accents indicate high tone—Navajo, like Chinese (and Ket) has tone on top of everything else—and *ł* is an *l* with a certain hissy friction from the sides of the tongue. This is *not* a language grown-ups have been picking up much!

Anyway, we assume that in a language actual people speak every day, these forms represent a pattern, as there would be in Spanish for *I buy*:

present	compr-**o**
past	compr-**é**
imperfect	compr-**aba**
future	compr-**aré**
subjunctive	compr-**e**

In Spanish a whole class of thousands of verbs like *comprar* work that way. But assuming that there are thousands of Navajo verbs that pattern like *lé* is wrong. Really wrong.

Compare our *move* verb to the same changes for the verb *cut out*, and you see that there is no similarity:

	move a rope-like thing	cut out
present	lé	géésh
past	lá	gizh
future	lééł	gish
repetitive	lééh	gish
subjunctive	lééł	géésh

And no, there's nothing special about the *cut out* verb—it's not "irregular" in any way that the *move* one isn't. So, we might think, there must be something like three verb classes as in Romance languages like Spanish, where there are *-ar* verbs like *comprar* and *-er* verbs like *comer*, "to eat":

I buy	compr-**o**	I eat	com-**o**
you buy	compr-**as**	you eat	com-**es**
he/she buys	compr-**a**	he/she eats	com-**e**

Wrong again. There was even a clue, in that the difference between the Navajo *lé* and *géésh* patterns seems to be more distinct than that between Spanish's *comprar* and *comer*. It looks like *lé* and *géésh* are just each doing their own thing, and they are—but not just them: it's every verb in the language! Here are some other perfectly normal verbs:

	move a rope	cut out	play	fill up with	dig out	chew	carry
present	lé	géésh	né	bin	gééd	'aał	teeh
past	lá	gizh	ne'	bįįh	geed	'aal	tį̂
future	lééł	gish	neeł	bį́į́ł	goł	'ał	tééł
repetitive	lééh	gish	neeh	bį́įd	go'	'ał	tééh
subjunctive	lééł	géésh	ne'	bin	gééd	'aał	tééł

There's no pattern that explains all of them, nor do they split into classes. Two forms are identical in two of the verbs—the future and repetitive are the same in *cut out* and *chew*. But you still can't know how the changes will work otherwise in either one—why is the vowel *i* instead of *éé* in three forms of *géésh* while it's *a* instead of *aa* in just two for *'aał*? Dim, halfway-there rules of thumb are all you get. There are no tables to learn, no lists of endings—because there *are* no rules.

It's a pain for English speakers to have to learn the gender of every noun in French or German along with the noun itself. But in Navajo, for every single verb in the language, you have to learn these five variations. You just have to know. The nearest equivalent for an English speaker would be if every verb were like *be*, where we have to know that it's *I am* but *I was* and *I've been* and, subjunctively, *if I were*—just imagine if English had it in addition that today I speak, yesterday I spoke, tomorrow I spock, repetitively I spack, and hypothetically I just might spoo.

The Navajo verbs that give you any real break—such as *work*, in which all five forms for no reason are just *nish*—are rare. Plus, I am oversimplifying in giving you only these five forms. Really you have to learn another five as well, depending on what nuance you are conveying *within* the five basic ones. The bit-by-bit-then-bang! trajectory with *stink* is done within one set of five, but if you're just talking about unnuanced reeking, period, then you use the "default" five forms. We don't need to see them. Suffice it to say that some of the default forms are identical to the nuanced ones, but only some. For each verb, you just have to know which ones are. As well as which aren't. And for those that aren't, what *their* forms are.

Asked point-blank to give an English word, you'll probably come up with a noun. House. Dog. Okapi.* If you wanted to teach someone English, the first thing you'd be inclined to impart would be the names of things, à la Adam and Eve. You don't start someone out with *lift* or *think*. But language is every bit as much about verbs. Human beings of lasting interest to other ones are not given to going about calling out the names of things. To say anything worth hearing, you have to express what things do, and that requires a verb. Talking is all about

---

* Well, you should. They're deeply beautiful animals, basically coffee-brown giraffes with normal necks, big ears, and white stripes on their haunches, unknown to Westerners until 1901. I have a little plastic model of one. I sponsored one at a zoo; he would reach out with his long purple tongue and take leafy branches I would feed him. He had a white patch on his nose. He died. They got a new one.

verbs—and in Navajo, all of them are irregular. Navajo is running irregularity. The word *Navajo* means "Irregularity runs through it."

Oh, of course it doesn't—but it should. Our perception of language is that the heart of it is "the grammar," regular patterns to be memorized—e.g., this kind of thing below for French, in which I am imitating the hoarier self-teachers I am just old enough to have encountered on their last legs in libraries in the seventies (anybody remember the old Hugo books, for example?):

Present Tense

je parle	I speak	nous parlons	we speak
tu parles	you (sing.) speak	vous parlez	you (pl.) speak
il/elle parle	he/she speaks	ils/elles parlent	they speak

(N.B. In colloquial parlance, the form *on* is often used in the first person plural; it is also used in the impersonal; see 125e.)

Future Tense

je parlerai	I shall speak	nous parlerons	we shall speak
tu parleras	you (sing.) shall speak	vous parlerez	you (pl.) shall speak
il parlera	he shall speak	ils parleront	they shall speak

Certain irregular forms must be learnt separately; see 128d.

Grammar under this conception is a series of patterns impartable via "Repeat after me" tutelage, and then there are scattered irregularities to be "learned separately."

But Navajo doesn't submit to this kind of treatment: all the verbs must be learnt separately, as it were. And yet this language has served its speakers quite well for millennia: for whatever it's worth, it has the most speakers of any Native American language above Mexico (about 140,000), and it did help us win a war.

It leads to a question: is it really so important that a language "make sense" in the way that we are told? Does Navajo, with its verbs that all go their own way, give the appearance of being undeveloped in relation to English—or does it seem, rather, more developed? Perhaps *fiercer*, as the young'uns are saying these days?

In any case, the truth is that English speakers handle more irregularity than we tend to think much about—to an extent that shows that language is all about chaos just as the Navajo situation does. Because we've handled English's mess since toddlerhood, to us it just "is," but if English were spoken by a village tribe in the Amazon, and the Chinese had inaugurated linguistic documentation, then they would describe our verbs in terms perhaps less astounded than mine about Navajo's, but astounded nonetheless.

Think about our past tense marking: the rule is that you use -*ed* (*walked*), but then there are cases that must be "learnt separately" like *see, saw*. However, there are quite a few of these "cases"—i.e., they're most of the verbs we use most often, and there are, at best, rules of thumb. If it's *see, saw*, then there was that time your toddler *paw* in his pants, right? If I think now and thought yesterday, then I assume that yesterday I *drought* a glass of wine and in 1912 a collision with an iceberg *sought* the *Titanic*. And then there are other exceptions that only become clear when we think of sound rather than spelling. *Bite, bit*, so *fight, fit*, right? But no, *fit* only happens in dialects considered "mistaken"! Meanwhile, we now have *light, lit*—but until not so very long ago, *lit* was considered vulgar in polite company and grammarians urged *lighted*. In *The House of Mirth*, Edith Wharton has Ned Van Alstyne casually coo, "Fifth Avenue is so improperly lighted."

Moreover, these forms always change over time, from place to place, and even from person to person. *Dove* has only become default of late; back in the day people *dived* into lakes and rivers. Most of us now (in America) would say *snuck* rather than *sneaked*, but that, too, is newish—and quite highly irregular, as it's not based on any pattern. I have never observed that a roof *luck* after a storm and *wruck* havoc on the shingling. Or, if I snuck, then if I talked with someone that day I *spuck*. But I didn't.

This is the way it is with a good 175 verbs in English, if you also count the ones that don't change at all in the past, like *beat* and *put* (that's irregular, too). This is distinctly unorderly: languages have messy hair.

IRREGULARITY: SITUATION NORMAL

But not because anybody wills it that way. It's an inevitable result of the fact that language is always changing—not just in words replacing one another (e.g., no more *thou*) but in the grammar itself changing (e.g., no more -*st* verb ending that went with the *thou*, either). The changes happen bit by bit, below the level of consciousness, taking one bite after another out of patterns and leaving gashes. Irregularity is especially inevitable because so many different kinds of changes are always buffeting the language from various directions. Collisions are inevitable.

German has a suffix, -*chen*, that makes things dear and small—*Liebchen* means, roughly, "love-ling," *Gretchen* started as "little Greta dear"—and it has neuter case. That means it takes the article *das* instead of the masculine *der* or feminine *die*. *Dog* is masculine—*der Hund*—but make it little and cute as a puppy and it's *das Hündchen*. But once that suffix exists, you just know that somewhere along the line, -*chen* will be applied, quite logically, to a woman to create a word meaning something like *girly* or *maiden*. It was: *Mädchen*. But that meant, automatically, an irregularity—*das Mädchen* is a neuter word even though it refers to something clearly female.

Or, if one way of marking the plural in the parent to all of the Germanic languages, Proto-Germanic, was -*i*—and it was—then you just know that in pronunciation, that -*i* will start having an effect on the vowels that come before it. So the plural of *man*, pronounced "mon" in this era, was *mani* "mahnee." The *ee* sound is pronounced in the front of the mouth, while the *ah* sound is in the back (try saying *ee-ah-ee-ah* and notice how you switch forward and back). After a while, anticipating the upcoming *ee*, speakers started pronouncing the *ah* more frontally. One way of doing that is to pronounce it *eh* (say *eh-ee-eh-ee* and everything stays up front). This meant that "mahnee" was now pronounced "meni." But sounds have a way of dropping off the ends of words as a language moves along—think about all of those now-silent *e*'s in English and French. The plural *-i* marker was no exception, and so by the time Proto-Germanic was Old English, *meni* was just *men*. Voilà, an irregular plural: singular *man*, plural *men*. That's how that kind of thing happens.

And this is not something local to Germanic or European languages, nor is irregularity solely a matter of what happens to endings. The same kinds of things happened with Chinese classifiers. We must be under no impression that they divvy up nouns so neatly that there's one classifier for all flat things and one for all animals and so on.

Example: the "skinny" one, *tiáo*, applies also to things like issues and affairs, as in *sān tiáo xīnwén*, "three news items." Why? How are the issues of the day skinny? If anything, they would intuitively seem rather portly. But in China's antiquity, business matters were written on strips of paper—skinny, of course—such that it was natural to refer to them as "skinnies," too. Today, by extension, *tiáo* is used to refer to "items" even discussed in the abstract with no physical form, and you just have to know.

Or, while *tiáo* applies to certain skinny things, the animal classifier *zhī* moonlights as applying to other skinny things—usually ones more like a stick: *sān zhī jiàn*, "three arrows"—such that to speak Mandarin requires knowing which skinny things take *tiáo* and which ones take *zhī*. It's because when it was used to mean "unit," *zhī* often referred to one of the things that occurred in pairs—such as legs. Legs are skinny, and from there it felt natural to use *zhī* to refer to things like arrows. Over time, *tiáo* glommed on to some skinny things while *zhī* glommed on to others. No Chinese speaker has any way of knowing that now—they just have to know when it's *tiáo* and when it's *zhī*.

Then in many cases the reason for the kink today is unknown. While *zhāng* is usually used for flat things, *běn* is used for books. Given that *běn* began as a word for *root*, we will likely never know why it came to apply to what you're holding. What we do know is that Mandarin classifiers present the same random exceptions as Romance languages do with cases like the *hand* word, which "should" be masculine but which you learn is actually feminine. In Spanish this means that *mano* takes *la* despite its masculine -*o*. In Mandarin it means that *horse* takes its own classifier *pǐ* instead of *zhī*.

In any case, irregularity happens, one randomly logical yet disruptive step at a time. Language change first creates patterns, like a list of classifiers used with nouns according to shape. But then the language keeps changing. That can mean that the system gets more ingrown—more classifiers. That can also mean that the system starts getting dissheveled—classifiers applied to nouns for no reason any longer perceptible. Of course, most often the two things happen at the same time.

TO BE A LANGUAGE, THEN, is to be a mess, and the only question is to what extent. As you might suppose, irregularity decreases to the extent that adult learners have smoothed it out over time. This means that a hideous amount of irregularity is, like an equal amount of ingrownness, the default state of language. User-friendliness is an accident.

In Archi, even the word for something as particular and random as the corner of a sack has a completely irregular plural: one corner of a sack is *bič'ni* while several are referred to as *boždo*! Today English has a handful of plurality wrinkles like *man, men* and *person, people*. But in Old English, before the Viking impact, they were more prolific. A literate person had shelves groaning under the weight of what would now be pronounced as *beek*, while goats were *gæt*, oaks were *æc*, and dungeons were *ding*. Pashto is shot through with irregular plurals on top of the regular ones. The plural of *mother, mor*, is *maynde*, and *son* and *daughter* are *zoy* and *lur*, while *sons* and *daughters* are *zāmən* and *lurîe*. With these and quite a few others, as with so much else in Pashto, you just have to know.

It's this kind of thing that adult learners don't handle well. It's easy to put yourself in the head of one of the people who made Persian less irregular than Pashto, or English less irregular than Navajo. In a bilingual city like New York, one hears people saying ¡*No me digas!* "You don't say!" and *Ya te dije . . .* "I told you . . ." all the time, using two irregular forms of the verb *say*, whose infinitive is *decir*. In a place where people spent their whole lives speaking messy, makeshift Spanish, that kind of thing—*digas* and *dije* for a verb whose default form is *decir*— would be one of the first to go.

In the same way you can almost predict, from Modern Standard Arabic, what didn't make it into the local Arabics. In Arabic, as in its relatives like Hebrew, the numbers from three to ten take nouns of the "wrong" gender. *Three* is *talāta* in the masculine and *talātat* in the feminine. But you say *talāt-u banāt*, "three girls," and *talātat-u awlād*, "three boys." It's just that way, but as one Web site breezily puts it, when it comes to this grammatical twist, "Most Arabic natives make mistakes or simply don't care." If it's hard even for them, then surely adults in Morocco with native languages of their own would have felt the same way learning Arabic by ear. Apparently they did: a Moroccan number used with a noun doesn't even have different genders.

THE INHERENT MESSINESS OF LANGUAGE, and the fact that it can exist to such extremes with the sky not falling in, leads to a question about English and the sense of what "rules" are supposed to be. Namely, one might ask: why can't there be irregular pronouns?

Our idea that English is typical of how languages work is only because we speak it and learn little about what "normal" languages like Archi and Navajo are really like. Equally arbitrary is our sense that it's normal for a language to have irregular verbs, and even irregular nouns, but sinful for it to have irregular pronouns.

The French have no problem with:

Guillaume	et	moi	sommes	allés au	magasin.
William	and	me	are	gone to	the store

where anyone who tried to use the regular subject form of the pronoun *je* in place of *moi* would likely be fined. That's simply considered an irregularity, alongside French's typical array of irregular verbs, in a language its speakers are intensely proud of. If it's good enough for the French, and Navajo can get along without even a single regular verb, then we English speakers need to get over *Billy and me went to the store*.

No one says "You should say *thinked*—that's the rule, past tense is marked with *-ed.*" The only reason no one says that is because we never hear anyone say it. Before a certain coterie of people seeking to spruce up English so that it could take its place as a world language started complaining about things like *Billy and me* in the eighteenth century, no one heard anyone complaining about irregular pronouns, either.

If a Navajo can talk about stinking in five irregular ways, surely we can put up with Billy and me going to the store, as well as each student handing in *their* paper.

THE ROT IN EVERY LANGUAGE

Navajo also rattles with things that started as living grammar but now have no meaning at all and would qualify, heard by someone speaking earlier Navajo, as "mistakes." In this, English is also much more like Navajo than it can seem, such that Navajo has a lesson to teach us about what "proper" grammar is—or should be thought to be.

For example, Navajo has a prefix that can turn a verb that is about an experience into one about having an effect on something. In English we have, for instance, *rise*, which is something that just happens to you, and *raise*, which is making something rise. In the same way, something can just be a-boil, but it can also be that someone is boiling the something. Navajo can mark that difference explicitly with a prefix, our hissy little variation on *l*, *ł*.

This means that you can start with:

Yi-béézh "It's boiling"

and plunk in the *ł* to make a new meaning:

Yi-ł-béézh "He's boiling it."

Then there's another prefix that can make a verb with that kind of *ł* in it passive. This time the prefix is *l*—which to a Navajo speaker is as different from *ł* as *b* is from *p* for us. So, if *He's drying it* is *Néi-ł-tsááh* then to say *It's being dried* you say *Ná-l-tsááh*.

This looks like something about Navajo that would submit to tabulation in the good old-fashioned way, learnable like Latin:

> To render a verb transitive the prefix -*ł* is used; to render the passive the prefix -*l* is substituted

and so on. But teaching Navajo that way wouldn't be honest—these prefixes actually only serve those functions occasionally.

With countless verbs, the -*ł* prefix has to be used, as obligatorily as a stamp on an envelope, even though they aren't about doing anything to anybody or anything. With the verb root *ti'* for *talk* plus assorted prefixes that need not concern us, *yéíní-ł-ti'* means "you talked," but even though you have to include the *-ł*, *talk* isn't a verb like *boil*. You boil an egg, but you don't talk your grandmother. The *-l* "passive" prefix, meanwhile, pops up all over the place with no passiveness implied in the least. That *work* verb *nish* has to be preceded by an *l*: *nada-l-nish* is *they work*, but nothing like the nonsensical *they were worked*. The *géésh*, "cut out," verb also has to be used with the *-l* prefix, for no reason.

The fact is that in *most* cases, *-ł* and *-l* come for free without adding any meaning. They are just stuff along for the ride that you have to know to include. What this means is that in Navajo there *are* verb classes like Spanish's *-ar/-er/-ir* ones in a sense, depending on whether they drag along a usually meaningless *-ł*, *-l*, or, in other cases, a *-d* prefix I have refrained from describing,* or in still other cases nothing at all. *Gééd*, "dig out," and *'aał*, "chew," from the table above are nudists, and they have a lot of company.

But because these prefixes do have a purpose sometimes, they have double lives. They are both meaningful, where *-ł* indicates doing something to something as in *yi-ł-béézh* "he's boiling it," and meaningless, where *-ł* is just something that makes the *talk* verb part of an *ł*-class where *ł* is just some mute bit of stuff: *yéíní-ł-ti'*, "you spoke." And they are meaningless more often than not. That is, ask a Navajo what *ł* means in *yéíní-ł-ti'*, and she'll say that it "just is." It's random.

We can assume that *ł* didn't start that way: it's something that happens in a language over time. There must have been a time when *ł* actually did always make a verb mean that you're

---

* Because, Navajoists, morphophonemic rules (i.e., dear readers, the kind that make us change sounds in narrow contexts, such that we say one *leaf* but two *leaves* when *-s* is a plural marker, but when it's a third-person-singular marker, we say *He quaffs beer* rather than *He quavves it*) so often leave the *-d* changed or off that it would require a hideous digression about something as reader-unfriendly as rule-ordering to demonstrate its usage, and all for a prefix that has (when it has one) a passivizing function similar to that of *-l*.

doing something to something, just like in English, -ed always puts a verb into the past. If we could ask an ancestor of the Navajo woman some thousands of years ago what *ł* meant, then that person could have said, "What? It means that you're doing something to something," because it always did. But as time passes, words' meanings change and slip away from what their prefixes and suffixes originally meant. Did it ever occur to you that the verb *kneel* has *knee* in it? The *l* at the end started, believe it or not, as the same suffix that words like *spittle* and *curdle* have. *Spittle* is about spit jiggling about, *curdle* is about curds made to jiggle about: *-le* is about jiggling about (think *giggle, fondle, wiggle*). *Kneel* started out as meaning "to knee-le," as it were— jiggle those knees down to the ground. Who'd know now? The *l* is no longer a suffix; it's just a sound. Navajo's *-ł* and *-l* are a long way down that road.

But what that means is that Navajo verbs, on top of their maddeningly senseless variation from tense to tense, usually come also with a grace note of junk.

AND YET NAVAJO, despite this shambolic, unruly disshevelment at its very core, is the linguistic equivalent of the Nôtre-Dame Cathedral, an awe-inspiring, kaleidoscopic, Pollockian splash of a thing. People actually *speak* Navajo! And it doesn't even hurt! If anything, to strike a messy subjective note, the junk is plain fun—added complexity, remnants of history, more crags. More *real*.

It leads to a question: if a language can be as shamelessly messy as Navajo and yet remain a mighty, remarkable construct, then where does that put the traditional insistence that English keep dying constructions in iron lungs for purposes of clarity or logic? Why can't English get sloppy?

We tell people they have "made a mistake" in saying *I was just laying there* because one is to use *lie* in such a context, laying being something you exert. If it was good enough for Anglo-Saxon shepherds, then it should be good enough for us. And then meanwhile we hear younger people saying "He's all . . ." instead of *He said . . .* and wince at this intrusive "slang," which "isn't right" because, well, it wasn't familiar to the people who used to keep *lie* and *lay* separate? That Shakespeare spoke a different English from Chaucer is considered luscious. That people fifty years from now might speak slightly differently from us is considered a herald to the demise of civilization as we know it.

From the underwater perspective on language, this obsession with keeping English the way it used to be and treating new constructions as peeves looks like someone up on the beach trying to keep the shoreline dry with a towel. All languages are full of detritus from things that have changed beyond recognition unmourned—or, put another way, language change is an ongoing procession of mistakes. Modern English became Old English via hundreds of "mistakes." It is this kind of thing that is behind much of the Richard Lederer "Why don't we grieve a greption" kind of observation, but it goes far beyond it to things we don't even notice. In brief, English is already splattered with mess.

Suppose instead of interviewing that Navajo woman, we interviewed none other than you. Let's say we asked you how to turn an adjective into a noun. What would most likely come to your mind would be the suffix *-ness*: *happy* is an adjective, *happiness* is a noun. *Red, redness. Sad, sadness.*

Okay, but how would you turn the adjective *warm* into a noun? *Warmness*? Not really. You would say *warmth*. And how did you do that? With the *-th* suffix. But it never occurs to most of us that there even is a *-th* suffix, even though it's all over the language. Think about it: *warmth, growth, width, strength, breadth, youth, death, birth, health, wealth,* and on and on. All of these words refer to a process or a quality, and what they have in common—i.e., what in them conveys that meaning—is *-th*.

Yet we don't think of it that way, and that's because it's dead. It's dead in the sense that we can't make new words with *-th*. The use of *gross* to mean *disgusting*, for example, is only several decades old, but we can now also say *grossness* (but not *grossth*). One of my favorites lines in the musical *Hairspray* (stage version) is when Penny Pingleton, somewhat hesitant of expression, consoles protagonist Tracy Turnblad about ending up in the special education class and ventures, "Tracy, I'm sorry about your special ed . . . *ness*!" That one is a joke, but we can even use it on the fly without it being a joke: is *grayness* an actual word? If it isn't, it still doesn't sound wrong to append -*ness* to *gray*. Little -*ness* is a living piece of grammar, a part of how we express ourselves in the language. In comparison, -*th* is a fossil.

Not only would we not say *greenth*, but we'd have to work to process what it even meant—and not because it would be too hard to pronounce: we say words like *fifteenth* all the time. Nor would we try *oldth** or *shallowth*. Part of why we don't actually use -*th* anymore is that usually, the sounds in its words have changed so much that we can barely manage to connect them with the original root if at all. Cases like *warmth* and *growth* are the exception. With *width*, *strength*, *length*, and *breadth* we have a faint awareness of their origin in *wide*, *strong*, *long*, and *broad*. But with *youth* and *birth*, to hear that they are related to *young* and *to bear* elicits an "Oh, yeah . . . !" Meanwhile the roots that yielded *wealth* and *health* are now words so antique they're barely words anymore: *weal* as in *the common weal* and *hale* as in *hale and hearty* (but note we would never say "I work out three times a week to keep *hale*"). Finally, there are cases that are completely opaque, such as *sloth*, which started as *slowth*, and *mirth*, which had its roots in what became *merry*. *Filth* is another one— we can say *grossness* but not *foulth*, unaware that *filth* is the result of *foul* plus -*th* after millennia of sound change.

---

* Actually, the Viv character in an early episode of Lucille Ball's sitcom after *I Love Lucy*, *The Lucy Show*, did, contrasting *oldth* with *youth*. But it was intended as a joke, which is my point. I mention this because you'd be surprised how particular people get who write you after reading your books. I could not have it thought that I didn't buy the DVD set of the first season of *The Lucy Show* as soon as it came out. There are certain priorities in this thing called life, after all.

The -*th* used to be very much alive—in Proto-Germanic it was a haler, heartier little -*itho* (now written as -*iþō*) applied as freely as -*ness* is now—one could speak of what in English would now be *lame-th* or *half-th*. The *i* part of -*iþō*, in fact, screwed up the vowels that came before it in the same way as *i* created irregular plurals like *men* from *mani*, which is why there are so many cases like *filth* instead of *foulth*. But things change.

In the first few *Thin Man* movies, which began in 1934, just before the Production Code starched up American cinema grievously for the next thirty-five years, Nick Charles is a heavy drinker and it's all presented as a joke. But by the fifth entry in the series, *The Thin Man Goes Home*, it's 1944. The studio that made the films, MGM, had settled into a homey all-American ethos most emblematically embodied by the Andy Hardy movies. This fifth Thin Man entry therefore has dear small-town character types like Harry Davenport and Gloria De Haven hanging around, and in this world, knocking back serial highballs is not considered funny. Thus in *The Thin Man Goes Home*, Nick drinks a lot of apple cider. Now, it's still the beloved Thin Man series, within which certain elements were basic and expected by audiences, and so some references are made to Nick and Nora drinking in the past. Or, there's a cute moment when Nora thinks Nick went out drinking the night before and complains to herself the next morning about Nick "sneaking off like that and getting drunk . . . without me!"

Very 1934, and the only such thing in this movie. It's something dragged along from the past because certain patterns had been set then. But if the series had begun in 1944, then the Charleses wouldn't have been drinkers at all. Nora's comment in *The Thin Man Goes Home* is the cinematic equivalent of -*th*.

We use -*th* words because they were up and living at one time. Now they are tokens of the past. If elderly, wet, and sitting in a stranger's living room being asked how English makes nouns, we would never put -*th* on a piece of paper. Poor -*th* is like a papery old abandoned wasp nest that you kick along for a spell as you stroll down a country lane (or the backlot where they filmed *The Thin Man Goes Home*). It's a dead thing—*and we use it all the time.*

The suffix -*some*, which creates adjectives, is similar. Again, we barely think of it as a suffix, because it can't be added to new words, even though *handsome, awesome,* and *wholesome* are everyday words and *gruesome* is not exactly obscure. The suffix shows its age, like -*th*, in that in many cases, the language has changed beyond the roots it is stuck to. *Handsome* is not the state of having hands (it started as meaning good with one's hands, and then a notion set in that men with that skill were probably attractive, and here we are now), and something ugly doesn't evoke *grue* in anyone.

To the extent that deadness can be thought of as occurring to degrees, -*some* is less dead than -*th*, because one can use it in a jocular sense. Or at least my wife and I do—*ugsome* and *shitsome* are, in our house, pretty much actual words. But only pretty much—and I don't expect the *stinksome* I snuck (sneaked?) in earlier in this chapter to ever catch on. English speakers drag -*some* along as a souvenir of an earlier stage in the language when there actually were words like *ugsome* (which there were). It's a kink in the system, a disshevelment one might say.

And such things are not just a matter of little suffixes—we use roots, robust chunks of actual wordness, all the time that have no meaning in themselves. Cranberries seem such a familiar thing, but what's a cran?* Just what is the cob that makes cobwebs? ("Help, a *cob!*") My favorite time of day is late afternoon and twilight—but I couldn't tell you what it means for the light at that exquisite time to be "twi." Or: *commit, submit, permit, transmit*—you know what those words mean, and that all of them have prefixes: *com-, sub-, per-, trans-*. But why can't you use

---

* In response to a cavil that gets around claiming that linguists are hoaxing the public by describing *cran-* as opaque, the issue here is not whether etymologists can figure it out. Of course they can; here the source is a Low German word for *crane*. However, the Anglophone home in which Low German is the language of choice is vanishingly rare, and in fact an oxymoron. Hence to the ordinary English speaker *cran* has no meaning.

mit alone, and if you did, what would it mean? And while we're on the subject, at what point in your life have you ever stretched, walked outside, taken a deep breath, and *ceived*? We conceive, receive, deceive, perceive—but somehow, we never get around to smelling the roses and just simply ceiving. And more to the point, if we decided to, just what activity would we engage in?

It's quite messy, this thing called English. Words and meanings don't match up nearly as nicely as we like to suppose, because the vocabulary is like a plant with dead leaves scattered throughout. In other words, I might say that a language is never sheveled—but then I can't say that, because the word doesn't exist despite the fact that, by all rights, it should, as should *kempt*. One cannot be *couth*—or, one seems rather the opposite if one utters it, nor can one show *ruth* to one's enemies, except under the peculiar circumstance of seeking victory over a foe by revealing to them the visage of someone named Ruth.

ENGLISH IS ALSO FULL of sounds that hover between life and death in terms of conveying meaning. For example, we have our own version of Navajo's largely fossilized *ł*. I likened it to how *rise* differs from *raise*, in which the key is the change from the *i* to the *ai* sound instead of the insertion of an *ł*. That is not, however, an isolated case in English. *Lie* and *lay* differ in the same way: the *ay* sound (spelled differently but it's the same sound as *ai* in *raise*) is what makes the difference between something just lying there and something being made to lie there, *laid* down. These two cases are remnants of what was once living grammar, where you turned an inert meaning into one about control by changing the vowel. It's why you can *fell* a tree (making it fall), it's why you can *set* something down (making it sit), and it's why to drench something is, in a manner of speaking, to make it drink, although that meaning has drifted quite a bit over the centuries.

But no one would put these pairs on a blackboard today outside of a linguistics class, because it's in ruins, scattered and irregular. There was a time when it stood mighty and strong. Back in Proto-Germanic, you could add that jolt of control to any verb where it would make sense. It started as a -*yan* suffix (written -*jan* today): *brennan* was to be burning, but *brennjanan* was to set something on fire (i.e., make it burn), and to make something fall was *falljanan*. What led to today's *fell* was anticipation, of all things. It has a major effect on how a language changes, and with these verbs, speakers knowing that the *y* was coming would subconsciously shape their tongues a little differently in pronouncing the verb's vowel before it. Thus the way was paved again for the same process that created *men* as the plural of *man*. Hence *fall/fell*, *drink/drench*, or in Proto-Germanic, *beitanan* for *bite* and *baitjanan* for putting a bridle on something (making it bite).

However, ask an English speaker what the *e* in *drench* "means" and he's in no better a place to answer than the Navajo woman asked why there's an *ł* in the word for *you spoke*, *yéínítti'*. In fact, the English speaker would have exactly as much to say about *drench* as he would about *yéínítti'*!

Then there are other little orphan curds beflecking our language, sounds that started as whole words in ways we would never even consider now. The *b* in *about* is all that's left of the *by* in what was originally *by-out*, with the *a* starting as *at* and tacked on later. That is: *about*, with five letters, comes from three words. The *l* in *lonesome* is a remnant of what started as *all*. *Alone* was first *all one* and was gummed together into *alone*. *One* was originally pronounced "oh-nuh," but when that changed to today's "wun," people stopped perceiving the -*one* in *alone*—"all-oh-nuh" at first—as being the word *one*. It now felt like if you were to divide *alone* into two pieces, then it would be not al-one but a-lone. The *a*- felt like something akin to the one in *akin* or *astride*, leaving *lone* as the root—one that hadn't existed before. *Lone* is *one* with a ripped-off tail end of *all* hanging on its windshield. It began as an expression, a neologism—surely something people would have written into newspapers complaining about if there had been any at the time.

This is only one of countless arrant mistakes that, if we were to reverse them, would deprive us of things we now consider eminently normal. Let's go back to Wharton's *Ned* Van Alstyne. Did you ever wonder why *Ned* is the nickname for *Edward*, *Nellie* for *Ellen*, and *Nan* for *Ann*? After all, if someone's name is Maria and you come to be fond of her, your impulse is not to start calling her N'Maria—and speakers of Old and Middle English were no sillier than we are. In itself, even *Ned* for *Ed* seems a little goofy—"Hey there, Ed, Eddie boy, good ol' . . . Nnnnned!!!" Why??? Today, if we have a friend named Aisha, the last thing we would start saying is "Ooh, here comes my . . . *Nnnaisha!*" What was it with early Brits and *n*?

The answer is a "mistake." Just as in German *my* is *mein*, in Old English *my* was *mīn*. You would say, in modern parlance, *mine book, mine cat*. And, you would often say, in affection, *mine Ed, mine Ellie*. As *mīn* changed to *my*, people started hearing the old *n* as the first sound in the names: *mine Ed* became *my Ned*. The result was new versions of these names starting with *n*, used as nicknames—i.e., names you use in affection, as people used to in saying *mine Ed.**

For a related reason, properly, there are no *notches*—the word is a mistake. There should be *otches*, as that was the original word. *Notch* happened when people heard *an otch* so often that they started thinking of it as *a notch*. Equally vulgar, if this was a "mistake," is a statement that Ned is Van Alstyne's nickname, since we "should" be talking about his "ickname"—*a nickname* happened when people misheard *an ekename*. *Newt*, to the extent that we ever say it ("Look, honey, a newt!"), is "wrong" for the same reason—it "should" be an *ewt* or, as it was at first, an *eft*, which is an actual word for the same slimy little

---

* Characters on the nineties Britcom *Keeping Up Appearances* conversationally refer to their sister Hyacinth as *our Hyacinth* regularly (or, when one of the sisters' husbands, Onslow, is less enthused about something Hyacinth has done, *your Hyacinth*). This is the modern equivalent of people of ye olde dayes cheerily saying *mīn Edweard* in the days before television (quite a few days before, to be sure).

critter, although you're only likely to come across the word in crossword puzzles. The tragically slovenly nature of the human condition meanwhile nicked the *n*'s off of other words by mistaking their initial *n* as part of an *an*. *Apron* started as *napron*— a *napron* sounded like an *apron*, and after a while, *apron* it was. But if that's wrong, then *umpire, adder,* and *auger* would also have to be classified as gutter talk.

I'm afraid we also need to get over the idea that there is such a thing as a pea, a cherry, or sherry. All three are mistakes. One pea was at first a *pease*—that's why it's "pease porridge hot." Medieval English speakers didn't mean what we would mean with "peas porridge," as, once again, they weren't silly: they wouldn't call pea porridge "peas porridge" any more than we would ask for "apples pie." But you can easily see how *pease* was subject to misinterpretation. It sounded like a plural, and so people assumed that there was a word *pea*. Now, it would seem, there is.

Cherry is *cerise* in French and that's where we got the word, but that sounded plural, too, and pretty soon we were hearing people singing about how "I Gave My Love a Cherry," which to some at the time must have sounded like someone being handed two slices of cheddar and saying "Okay, but I'm on a diet so I'll just take one chee." And sherry was named as the wine of *Xeres* in Spain (in earlier Spanish the *x* was pronounced *sh*). But "I'll have a glass of sherries," as it came out in English, was ripe for misinterpretation as just *sherry*. Hence we now consider ourselves rather "too too" when we sip something that we refer to with, technically, an unlettered barbarism.

And finally, there are quite a few words that we pronounce the way we do only because it's the way they were spelled in Latin! My favorite of these is *perfect*, which starts as *perfectus* in Latin but has no *c* in French, where it's *parfait*. English borrowed the word from French, and to the Middle English speaker the word was *parfit* or *perfit*, as we would expect. Think Chaucer: in the Prologue of *The Canterbury Tales* he describes the "verray, parfit gentil knyght"—it certainly isn't that the *c* somehow emerged after that for no reason ("Prithee, let us pronounce it perfi-c-t owing to a sweetere sounde!"). But at various times in the previous millennium, some writers advocated spellings that preserved sounds that words had had in their Latin versions, these processed as "original" elements now lost, as if words were nitrate films from the teens and twenties decaying in canisters and given emergency preservation.

This meant that even French's *parfait* was "wrong" in missing that Latin *c*, and thus it was deemed proper to pronounce *perfit* in English as "per-fekt." Yet we would never say "cas-tul" for *castle* despite Latin's *castellum* or "muss-kul" for *muscle*.

The same thing put the *l*'s "back" into *soldier* (the Latin source was *solidum*) and *fault* (from Latin's *fallere*), and it's the only reason we pronounce them now. Time was that those words were pronounced "so-jer" and "fawt" even by those thought of as the most eloquent. However, a sense of insecurity set in for good about the pronunication of these particular words, and now we spontaneously pronounce them with a sound that was a natural part of them in a language now dead that we didn't actually borrow them from! In an alternate universe we'd be saying "dow-but" for *doubt*. French just has *doûte*; it's Latin that had *dubitare*, and on that basis the *b* was jammed back in on paper—but never made the transition to living speech (nor do we repay "deh-buts").

WHAT THIS ALL MEANS IS that the very fabric of the English language we speak without a care is full of meaningless chunks, bits of stuff that hover awkwardly between life and death, sounds that started out as the ends or beginnings of adjacent words, and even sounds that wouldn't be in the language at all anymore if a few people hadn't decreed that they hang around in scattered random instances. Take a sentence like this:

A **per**fect sherry at **twi**light **rai**sed **N**ed's spirits a **n**otch and **permit**ted him to **for**get **ab**out his heal**th**.

In bold are all of the parts that are dead, dying, opaque, or the product of what began as mistakes. The *per-* in *perfect* and *permit* is bolded because one would be hard-pressed to say what it actually means by itself: *perceive, permit, perfuse, perfect, perambulate, perform, permutation, perpetrate*—any single sense of *per* is vague at best. The *for-* in *forget* is similar: *forbear, forlorn, forbid, forgive, forgo, forsake, forswear*—there's no use even trying to get a sense of a single meaning, despite *The American Heritage Dictionary* giving it the old college try with "completely, excessively, especially with destructive or detrimental effect." What? Is forgetting a matter of getting something excessively with destructive effect? Excuse me, but in modern English *for-* might as well be *oink* for all the meaning it has.

Take away the splotches and dead ends and oinks and flubs, and the sentence looks like a cartoon character with cracked teeth after an accident:

A fe t sherr at light r sed ed's spirits a otch and ed him to get out his heal.

HOW BAD IS OUR ENGLISH? SOME QUERIES

Modern English, in this light, is truly awful Old English. Absolutely execrable Old English—sad, really. Yet obviously we don't think of it that way, and shouldn't. The question is where to draw the line, which occasions, as always, questions. Such as:

Does it make any sense whatsoever to treat the difference between *lie* and *lay* as "correct" rather than just allowing the language to go where it's trying to, in which *lie* and *lay* are synonyms (*Lie it right here, Just lay there for a while*)? There was a time when this kind of alternation was a regular piece of grammar in the language, applying to heaps of verbs, that no one could miss. Today it's just a toy on the floor in the dark for somebody to trip on. When you give your baby a bottle, you do not refer to yourself as drenching her. If it was okay for none other than Lord Byron to write "There let him lay" in 1812 (*Childe Harold's Pilgrimage*) then why is it an "error" when you use *lay* in the same way? And keeping *lie* and *lay* separate does not aid clarity: never have I heard someone say *I'm going to just lay here for a bit* and wondered desperately "But *what* is he going to lay? *What???*" And I most certainly have never wondered "*Who* is he going to . . ." Plus, let us pass silently by the notion that I would think to myself "Whom? Whom is he . . . ," and the absurdity of that speaks to the general silliness in resisting the language's moving on as all languages always have—in order to become what they are now as opposed to what they were in antique stages we would never seek to restore. No one in Milan walks around annoyed that people aren't speaking Latin.

Also to consider: if we are to maintain *lay* as distinct from *lie*, then for consistency's sake we have to use *set* in the same way: *The glass sits on the table, I set the glass on the table.* But notice that this usage of *set* has a vaguely rustic or quaint feel for many today. You're helping move a sofa and someone says "No, set it there"—doesn't "put it there" sound more natural and even a little more, as the Brits say, posh?

Lie and *lay* clearly "want" to just be words that mean the same thing. Call that unsystematic, but all languages have synonyms. Language is sloppy.

IF WE'RE NOT GOING BACK to icknames and otches, then what logic is there in hearing *a whole nother* as illegitimate? *N* isn't the only sound that has jumped the gap between words here and there in English—such things are a natural process, as with *s* here and there. We probably say *whale* instead of *squale* because of an original *s* that got sucked onto a preceding word. Latin had the original form, as *squalus,* descended from the Proto-Indo-European word *skʷal-o-*. At some point, something like *his squale* became *his whale* like *a napron* became *an apron.*

When we want to say *another* but reinforce it with *whole,* we think of *an other*—obviously what *another* "is"—and spontaneously place the *whole* after *a-* rather than *an-* because it's how English works. *Whole* starts with a consonant, the *h* sound, and consonants come after *a* rather than *an*. But that leaves *-nother* on the other end:

another
a-whole-nother

which we could just embrace as one more word born from the nifty *notch*/*nickname* process.

But no—"wrong," "nonstandard." But only because words like *notch* emerged when writing and literacy weren't common yet, such that people didn't have a sense that the way the language happened to be caught in the headlights when written down was the way it should, or could, be until the sun burns the planet to a crisp.

The tragedy of the lowdown status of *a whole nother* is that there is no legitimate version—one is supposed to just avoid the entire construction despite how naturally it comes to mind. "An whole other" would break the fundamental rule of how *a* and *an* are used, and thus feels like cracking an axle in a pothole (yes, I do believe that there are rules—the question is whether we should embrace "rules" whose observance in the days of old would have blocked the emergence of the English we speak today). *A whole another* is dopey, too, because it means having two *a*'s. One is expected to apply a patch and avoid *a whole nother* like a curse word—but does that really make sense when to some folks several centuries ago, *notch* and *nickname* "weren't words" either?

"HE'S ALL 'I'M GOING TO TELL YOUR MOTHER' and she's all 'No, you're not' and I'm all 'Why don't you two just stop it?'" Is all there is to say about this that it is messy, overheated kid speech upon which the proper judgment is "I don't like it"?

Here's what I mean about how mistakes today are grammar tomorrow. In English, we have only one verb that can give us a sense of what it would feel like to speak a language with European-style conjugation, or, as I noted before, Navajo. That verb is *be*. Ordinarily we make do with lonely little third-person-singular -*s*, but with the peculiar *be* verb, suddenly English is a normal European language—or, really, language in general—with a different form for every person:

I walk	I **am**
you walk	you **are**
he/she walks	he/she **is**

Plus if I *were* to speak in the past, I *was* and I've *been*! That's our one shot at being able to shrug at the foreign learner and say, "Hee hee, I've never even thought about that . . . it just is!" (as a Russian once told me about their stroke-inducing noun declensions *and their exceptions!*).

Well, if English were allowed to morph on its merry way and embrace its irregularities rather than have them fumigated against as unseemly, then humble, sloppy little "He's all . . ." could give us a little more "hee hee."

English Now	**English Much Later**
I'm all "Stop it!"	I **maw** hello.
You're all "Stop it!"	You **raw** hello.
He's all "Stop it!"	He **zaw** hello.

In the English of the distant future, speakers would have started hearing the sound before *all* as part of the word—a perfectly natural process, after all—and after a while people wouldn't even process the words as connected with *all*. *I'm all* would become *I m'all* and finally, with the *I* dropping off as is common, *I maw*. But you *raw*, while she *zaw*. These *maw* words would be, of all things, a new verb! It would be a new verb meaning "say."

And as time went by, its associations with high-involvement narratives of the sort teenagers use when using *all* would fade, just as *awesome* once referred to things like the Taj Mahal and is now used to refer to it turning out that parking will be free downtown on Tuesday (or that Navajo verbs are irregular). *Maw* would just mean "say," as in saying hello—but with different forms for *I, you*, and *he/she*. Hee *hee!*

That really is one way that a word can emerge—similar things created words we use all the time. You might think with *arrive* being one of those words we borrowed from French, that there is a Latin word *arrivare*. Yet look that up in a Latin dictionary and it's not there. *Arrive* started as a Latin idiom: *ad ripam* meant "to the shore," as in getting to the shore in a boat. In Casual Latin (often known as Vulgar Latin), *ad ripam* was turned into a verb idiomatically: *ad-ripare*. Just as people might say "Let's middle-aisle it" to mean get married, *adripare* meant "to 'to-the-shore' it." Sounds change, and by the time Latin was French, *adripare* had become *arriver*, surely once processed by a contingent of Ancient Romans as "not a real word," "vulgar" Latin indeed.

LANGUAGES ARE MESSY—it's part of being the end product of sound changes, drifting meanings, and words coming together to make new ones. What's new in a language is neither a mistake nor subject, in a logical sense, to condemnation as unlikeable. It is inherent to languages to be always gradually becoming other ones—and that, ladies and gentlemen, is never an orderly process.

CHAPTER THREE

LANGUAGE IS INTRICATE

At this late date I only remember two things about the party. One is the worst paella I have ever had by far. If the person who made it was seeking to reproduce as faithfully as possible the taste and consistency of papier-mâché, they triumphed mightily that night (maybe that is what he was going for!).

The other is a conversation I had with a woman who had just gotten back from a stint with the Peace Corps in Ghana. I asked her whether she had learned any of the local languages. She said that she had indeed learned some Twi and that it hadn't been hard to pick up since "it doesn't have grammar."

I knew what she meant. Twi is analytic, to return to that term from the first chapter—it's low on suffixes and prefixes. Therefore, none of this faces us in learning Twi:

Present Tense

je parle	I speak	nous parlons	we speak
tu parles	you (sing.) speak	vous parlez	you (pl.) speak
il/elle parle	he/she speaks	ils/elles parlent	they speak

(N.B. In colloquial parlance, the form *on* is often used in the first person plural; it is also used in the impersonal; see 125e.)

93

Future Tense

je parlerai	I shall speak	nous parlerons	we shall speak
tu parleras	you (sing.) shall speak	vous parlerez	you (pl.) shall speak
il parlera	he shall speak	ils parleront	they shall speak

It was a party, and so I didn't bother to dwell on the point, but I was struck by her idea that if a language doesn't have tables of endings to be "learnt," then it "doesn't have grammar." It was another underwater moment—grammar to a linguist is so very much more than conjugation and declension.

In fact, the difference between that woman's sense of what language is and mine affects how people process differences between dialects of the same language. Taught that grammar is variations on the way English works, we cannot help but miss the richness of a great deal of the speech around us—even when it's in English. We miss that, no matter what anyone is speaking, if they're speaking it fluently, then whether it's exotic, suffix-less, or even vulgar, it's also an awesome system anyone would find hard as nails to learn after the age of about fifteen. That is: all human language is *intricate*. It's a lesson best learned by starting with languages like, in fact, Twi.

TWI ARE NOT AMUSED: "NO GRAMMAR"?

I suspect, for example, that the woman had not had occasion to really get cozy with the language. Her impression that Twi is easy to pick up would have surprised European explorers of the west African coast centuries ago, faced with the task of communicating in such a language before anyone had written it or studied it. Languages with grammars similar to Twi's are spoken from what is today Guinea on down through Liberia, Ghana, Togo, and Nigeria. They are members of various subfamilies of the Niger-Congo family, which covers most of the African land-mass. The only shop-window member of the family in terms of global familiarity is Swahili, but its grammar is quite different from the Twi-style kind, as it is part of the massive Bantu sub-family that does things in its own way.

Willem Bosman, a Dutchman, commented in 1705 about his and his men's experience with what would have been Twi or a close relative:

> We can hardly hit the pronunciation. The sound of some
> words is so strange, that though we have often endeavored
> to express them with our European letters, yet we have never
> been able to do it. . . . Could the Negroes, as I have said,
> either read or write, we should be able to learn their tongues
> speedily by observing the letters which expressed each
> thing; but having no other assistance than the bare sound, I
> think 'tis folly to attempt farther.

Bosman wasn't having an easy time, then, despite the lack of *amo, amas, amat* lists. Note that he was most frustrated by the sound. Specifically, what was throwing him was that Twi, like Chinese, is a language where tone is as important in conveying meaning as vowels and consonants. To be unable to "hit the pronunciation" in Twi is more than just to have a cute accent. It means you're incapable of any but the most rudimentary of utterances and constantly popping up with unintended ambiguities and double entendres.

Here is a particular pair of underwater goggles to put on: graphically, the way linguists indicate tone is with accents. High tone is indicated with the forward-pitched one, and lòw tone is indicated with the backwards-pitched one. High-toned *e* is é, low-toned *e* is è. *Nota bene*: these have nothing to do with the *accent aigu* and *accent grave* familiar to many of us from French. Looking through those goggles, we can see how tones can con-vey key distinctions of meaning—i.e., the tones are grammar.

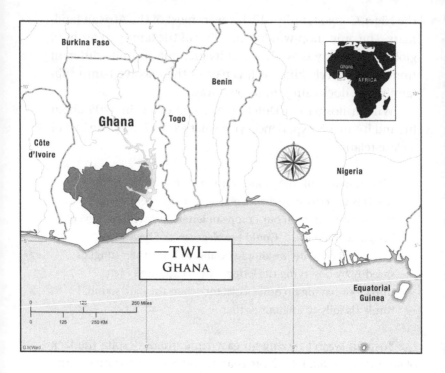

Here we go. Have you ever thought about the slight absurdity in saying that you "have" a head in the same way that you "have" a house? A house is something one gains and maintains possession of; a head is something you less possess than you just are. You can imagine a language in which people spoke of their relationship to their body parts in a different way than they spoke of their relationship to their furniture.

And while you imagine it, in countless places around the world people are doing it, and one of those places is Ghana. In Twi (specifically in the Asante dialect), possessive words like *my* have a different tone depending on whether you are talking about something like your umbrella or something like your butt. Namely, high tone for the umbrella and low tone for your butt—or, more delicately:

mé dáń "my house"
mè tí "my head"

Tone even indicates tense in Twi. The difference between
Kofi comes and takes it and *Kofi will take it* is not some ending or
little word, as we might expect, but just a difference between
low and high tone:

Kòfí bèfá "Kofi comes and takes it."
Kòfí béfá "Kofi will take it."

(Note also that it's not just vanilla present tense here, but
"comes and takes it"—nuanc-y, like Navajo's gradual stinking.
"No grammar" indeed!) Tone alone can even make a clause subordinate: when *rèbìsá,* "ask," has all high tones, it's subordinate:

Kòfí rèbìsá nó "Kofi was asking him"
Kòfí rébísá nó "while Kofi was asking him"

Twi clearly "has grammar." If Bosman and his men really felt
lost short of having someone to write out the sounds, then they
were never going to get much of anywhere—especially since
even in writing, how would anyone have written the tones?

A LESSON IN A LANGUAGE WITH "NO GRAMMAR"

Yet it is extremely tempting to suppose that a language is somehow
"primitive" when a language has no endings and you've grown up
speaking one that does. Wilhelm von Humboldt, erudite philoso-
pher and one of the founders of linguistic science, was the first
scholar to explicate the difference between analytic languages
and—here's another jargon term, which I promise not to use ever
again in this book—*synthetic* languages, ones that mash together

roots and prefixes and suffixes, like English does. He, in a time when facile rankings of "races" on a scale of "development" were fashionable, considered the development of prefixes and suffixes a mark of sophistication, with analytic languages representative of an initial, or even arrested, state. His verdict on Chinese was:

> Chinese structure, however we may explain it, is obviously founded on an imperfection in the making of the language, probably a custom, peculiar to that people, of isolating sounds, coinciding with an insufficient strength of the inner linguistic sense that calls for their combination.

That's laughable now, but it is instructive to put ourselves in von Humboldt's shoes. Imagine a language we don't know, spoken by people we've never heard of, and which has no conjugations or declensions, where words are mostly only one or two syllables long, maybe three. Who among us can truly say that we don't have even the slightest hint of a sense that this language is underendowed compared to one like Latin? Here is just such a language. We don't even need to know what this means:

Jà-the-jà hə hy ɣɛ ɔ́ njɛ̀ ɔ́ nɛ,
tjhu hỳ ɔ́ nɛ kṵ áŋ má láŋ ni ə̀ bi djɔ́ hɔ shá è,
tjɛ̀ bjṵ í má!

No endings. It looks like one short syllable after another, running by like cars on a choo-choo train. "Couldn't write *The Brothers Karamazov* in *that*," one might suppose—quietly, but still.

But to fully understand the marvel that all human speech is—that, to put a spin on Dr. Seuss, language is language, no matter how small—we might take a little lesson in this language. It's Akha, by the way, spoken in Thailand, Burma, Laos, Vietnam, and the south of China (by about 600,000, and yet no one's ever heard of it beyond where it's spoken; we live in a wide world indeed). Akha is a distant cousin of Chinese, a member of its family (called Sino-Tibetan, for the record).

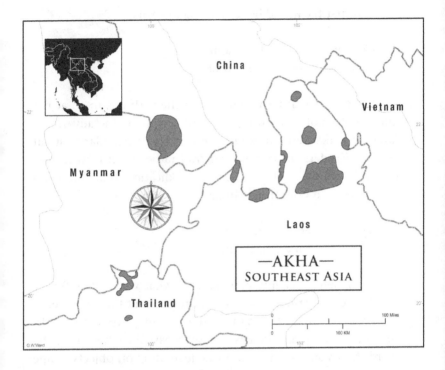

Here, in this language where you'll never have to be bothered with people asking whether you've "learnt" how to conjugate those irregular verbs, is your first assignment: say *I gave him one fruit*. Here are some words for you:

àjɔ̀ "he"
ŋá "I"
bì "gave"*
áshì "fruit"
thì "one"

---

* In Akha, a straight-up naked verb translates more readily as in past tense rather than present, when it's a verb about an action (like giving) rather than about a state of being (like liking). Therefore, *bì* "means" *gave* rather than *give*: the "-*ed*-ness" (to venture a different rendition of Penny Pingleton's *Hairspray* line) is built in. To make it mean *give* you'd have to add some things. Verbs tend to work like this in analytic languages.

Our first try would be something like this:

ŋà	bì	àjɔ̀	thì	áshì.
I	gave	he	one	fruit.

But the first thing wrong is that the verb has to go at the end. That's not something that only happens in "advanced" languages like German. And there's another particularity about the word order: *one* comes after *fruit* rather than before. *Fruit one*, not *one fruit*. This is our first indication that Akha has "grammar"—it does things in particular ways.

ŋà	àjɔ̀	áshì	thì	bì.
I	he	fruit	one	gave

Even here, you might sense that what we have is "crazy word order but still no *grammar* grammar." But there's more.

For one thing, Akha is in classifier country. Almost any self-respecting language in East or Southeast Asia has the little words that you use with numbers depending on objects' shape (roughly), and Akha is no exception. So *one fruit* (or *fruit one*) unadorned is wrong—you need your little counting word:

ŋà	àjɔ̀	áshì	thì	**shì**	bì.
I	he	fruit	one		gave

Then there's this *he*. Just because a language doesn't make something into an object—i.e., give it accusative case—with an ending, such as Latin's *puella* for *girl* and *puellam* for a girl "accused," doesn't mean it can't mark something as an object in some other way. Akha doesn't just make do with *he* no matter what. If *he* is an object, Akha can make it into a *him*, with a particle, and we need that, too:

ŋà	àjɔ̀	**áŋ**	áshì	thì	shì	bì.
I	he		fruit	one		gave

But this is still a baby way of saying *I gave him one fruit*. In Akha, if a verb is transitive (takes an object, as opposed to an intransitive verb, like *fall*), you have to mark the subject—not the verb—with a particle. Subjects that do things to something are different in Akha from subjects that just lay back and undergo something like falling or sleeping. Believe it or not, this kind of marking is very common in the world's languages, and Akha is one of them. We need that particle, too.

ŋà	**nɛ**	àjɔ̀	áŋ	áshì	thì	shì	bì̠.
I		he		fruit	one		gave

(Talk about "grammar," hee hee–style—you only use that particle in the *past* tense.) And then finally, to really make this a sentence anyone would say, there's a bit more. Akha has another particle that you add to the end of a sentence to lend a note of declaration. We do that with intonation; Akha has that, too, of course, but matches it with actual wordlets:

ŋà	nɛ	àjɔ̀	áŋ	áshì	thì	shì	bì̠	**ma**.
I		he		fruit	one		gave	

That, then—*ŋá nɛ àjɔ̀ áŋ áshì thì shì bì̠ ma*—is how you say *I gave him one fruit* in Akha, or in a more idiomatic sense, making it something you would actually contribute to a conversation, *I am the one who gave him one fruit*. Nine words to our five, encompassing all kinds of bells and whistles that barely translate into English but are clearly very much "grammar." This is stuff that would have to be "learnt."

In general, each Akha particle is a bulging piece of luggage: Akha can pack more into a particle than English often does into a whole sentence. To render a vanilla toss-off observation that someone is an Akha, you use a certain particle:

Àkhà **á**. "He's an Akha."

The *á* doesn't mean "he" and it isn't a *be* verb; it's just itself, a particle that connotes "is-ness." Now, never mind that the particle is different if it's me who is an Akha (*Àkhà é*); we'll stick with *he*. If you want to add some pepper, you use a different particle:

Àkhà **mέ**. "Yes, he is sure enough an Akha."

Put that in the past, and it's a different particle—different just in the tone!

Àkhà **mε**. "Yes, he sure enough was an Akha."

Ask a question, add a particle:

Àkhà mέ **ló**? "Is he an Akha?"

But it depends on the kind of question. Ask a question of the kind that anticipates agreement, and you use a different particle:

Àkhà mέ **là**? "He's an Akha, isn't he?"

Then, speaking Akha means being very explicit about how you know things. If you can see he's an Akha in his face, then that's a particle of its own:

Àkhà **ŋá**. "He's an Akha—I can see it."

If you can tell from his accent, then (yep!):

Àkhà **mía**. "He's an Akha—I can hear it."

And if it's just the kind of thing you can't quite explain but you know it when you know it, then yet another bit of stuff is required:

Àkhà á **nja**. "He's an Akha—I can feel it."

Akha, even without endings and such, is *intricate*, like any language.

One of my favorite other ways Akha is intricate is how it handles *very*. We might assume that having a single word *very* is all one might need. Maybe you can get a little more expressive and say *really* or *seriously* and then there are the slang versions (*wicked, mega, hella, mad*) that change every ten years or so, but *very* will always do, and what more do you need? Well, if you're Akha, a lot more: individual adjectives have their personal words for *very*, and you just have to know them. Now, that's grammar! The word for *very* comes *after* the adjective, and so if *blue* is *phý,* then *very blue* is *phý dù i* (the *i* marks it as an adverb—grammar again). One could even render the situation as something like:

The following forms must be learnt by rote (cf. Exercises in Appendix C):

nạ̈ **kha** i	very deep
pjhú **də̀** i	very white
phý **dù** i	very blue
ɣɔ̀ **lø** i	very big
bú **tjø**i	very clean

And while we're on it, there's that squiggle under many of the letters. That signifies one more thing about Akha—there's not only tone, but also you can pronounce a syllable with a slightly creaky vocal timbre, and that makes a difference in meaning, too.

ma	mother
má	full
mà	not
mạ	dream
mạ̀	group

Thus: say *ma* with a chirpish rise and it means "full"; say it with a hint of dejection and it means "not"; say it a little squawky and it means "dream"; say it with a hint of dejection *and* a dusting of squawkiness and it means "group."* The squawk alone can make the difference between something being for me or for others: *nḛ̀* for me, just *nè* for you.

In sum, there is nothing at all elementary about *Jà̰-the-jà hə hy ɣɛ ɔ́ njḛ̀ ɔ́ nɛ, tjhu hỳ ɔ́ nɛ ku̱ áŋ má láŋ ni ə̀ bi djɔ́ hɔ shá è,tjḛ̀ bjo̱ í má.* It isn't just words run together devoid of the "grammar" that case and conjugational endings lend a language. Akha has its own kind of grammar.†

WHAT CAN AKHA TEACH US ABOUT EBONICS?

This is an important lesson, that grammar is about more than things like French's *je suis, tu es, il est.* It puts us in a better position to feel better about what we hear around us on a regular basis. We will address Black English—perhaps better known as Ebonics these days. Is Black English "wrong"? If not, why?

---

* Akha specialists actually indicate the creaky vocal timbre by writing a *q* after the vowel, such that *mà̰* is *màq.* I'm breaking with that tradition here, in favor of using the more general strategy from the International Phonetic Alphabet of putting a tilde under the vowel like thi̱s. Specialists in languages from this part of the world have often used consonants to indicate things about the preceding vowel, such as tone, because it makes writing easier than if you have to keep stopping to add marks onto the vowel itself, and this was especially the case back in the day with typewriters. However, we've got word processing now, and I figured I'd spare you reading consonants as indicators of vowel color. Besides, the proliferation of *q*'s makes the language look vaguely fantastical given the marginal, "only-before-*u*-and-so-lots-of-points-in-Scrabble" status of the letter in English, whereas my goal is to show that even without conjugations and declensions, Akha is perfectly normal.

† This is reminding me of the talking walrus. The untranslated Akha sentence means, for whatever it's worth, "Catching wild boars being this big, having raised them to a size, I ask you to try to let them stay without keeping them in a pen, they'll run away."

Assorted researchers suppose themselves to have answered this question with an authority that ought to convince the public that Black English is a different, rather than a lesser, kind of English. They vary between weary and indignant to see that year after year the dialect is still thought of as "mistakes." However, between what we have seen in this chapter as well as the previous two, we are in a position to get what these researchers mean in a real way. Actually, we can get even more, because the case as usually presented leaves some things out that must be faced head-on to preach beyond the converted.

First, however, we have to be sure what Black English is. I refer not to black slang, which is rendered *in* Black English, but is used most copiously by just one age group (young) and changes constantly. To the linguist, Black English is how its words are put together and how they are pronounced. Put in another way, it is the dialect that the vast majority of black Americans speak, or can speak, to some extent regardless of age group, and namely, the aspects of it that stay the same over time or only change very slowly. There are citations of black Americans saying *be*-less sentences of the *She my sister* kind in the 1700s, for example, whereas we can be sure they weren't saying ____ (insert here some current black slang expression; experience has taught me that something being used at the moment I am writing will look glaringly archaic after about ten minutes).

So what I mean by Black English is—yes—what is commonly heard as "the mistakes," spoken by not only baggy-pants teens but dear old grandmothers. To be maximally clear, we will look at a gorgeously authentic sample of Black English, with almost all of the basic grammatical features that distinguish it from Standard English. That is, pretty much all of the classic "grammatical errors" are here. I try to avoid repeating examples from book to book, but I am making an exception for the Shirley story, which I used in a book long ago but which is just too perfect not to revive here (and frankly, only so many people have ever read that book!).

There's no slang here. If anything, the passage, written

around 1980, is getting a tad elderly. The characters today would neither be named Shirley and Charles nor do anything so antique as write letters. However, that's good in a way—it shows the eternal core of the dialect as opposed to the passing fashion of the slang.

It a girl name Shirley Jones live in Washington. Most everybody on the street like her, 'cause she a nice girl. Shirley treat all of them just like they was her sister and brother, but most of all she like one boy name Charles. But Shirley keep away from Charles most of the time, 'cause she start to liking him so much she be scared of him. So Charles, he don't hardly say nothing to her neither. Still, that girl got to go 'round telling everybody Charles s'posed to be liking her.

But when Valentine Day start to come 'round, Shirley get to worrying. She worried 'cause she know the rest of them girls going to get Valentine cards from they boyfriends. That Shirley, she so worried, she just don't want to be with nobody.

When Shirley get home, her mother say it a letter for her on the table. Right away Shirley start to wondering who it could be from, 'cause she know don' nobody s'posed to be sending her no kind of letter. So Shirley, she open the envelope up. And when she do, she can see it's a Valentine card inside, and she see it have Charles name wrote on the bottom.

So now everything going to be all right for Shirley, 'cause what she been telling everybody 'bout Charles being her boyfriend ain't no story after all. It done come true!

It a girl name Shirley Jones: *there('s)* becomes *it('s)* in Black English. *She a nice girl*: here is the famous absent *be* verb. *Shirley treat all of them*: third person singular *-s* can be left off. *Just like they was her sister and brother*: in the past, *was* can replace *were*.

'Cause she start to liking him so much she be scared of him—this *be* is very much "grammar," used to indicate something that happens on a regular basis. If Shirley saw a spider in the corner, one time, she would not say "I be scared of it." Even to those with only a passing familiarity with the dialect, all you need is a decent ear to sense that Shirley would sound a little minstrelly there, and it's because no black person would say it.

So Charles, he don't hardly say nothing to her neither—eek, double negatives; triple, in this case, actually. *The rest of them girls going to get Valentine cards from they boyfriends*: pronouns have their particularities in Black English—*them* is used as a demonstrative in place of *those*, and *they* can be used as a possessive in place of *their*. *She see it have Charles name wrote on the bottom*: English's irregular verbs are sometimes differently irregular (dissheveled) in Black English.

Plus Black English can leave off the possessive -*'s*, and so just *Charles name*, which is pronounced just like that, not as "Charleses name" as in Standard English. The black expression *baby mama* gets traced to Jamaican patois sometimes out of a sense that it's exotic in some way—but it's just Black English: *Charles name*, *Bebe kids* (if I may date myself a bit with a reference to the late black comedian Robin Harris's signature routine, enshrined in a delightful animated movie), *baby mama*. No one of any color is used to seeing nonstandard language on the page, and some don't recognize the absent possessive -*'s* as Black English—but just listen for it and you'll catch it before long (I have given the same advice to some who similarly question the use of *it's* for *there's*).

There is one thing the Shirley story largely leaves out, and it's that Black English is also about sound. Dialects differ not only on the level of grammatical constructions, but on how words are pronounced, and Black English is no exception. Most black Americans have, although it's not usually put this way, a different accent than Standard English speakers, which they use when speaking not only Black English but also standard—which is why several linguistic studies have shown that white and black Americans are very quick to distinguish whether someone is black even on the phone. Of course, we could also put it that Standard English speakers have a different accent than black speakers—the point is that there is indeed a "black sound." Not all black people have it, but most do to some extent, while the number of whites who have it is very small.

Thus it won't help to imagine the Shirley story intoned in the voice of an announcer over the credits of a fifties sitcom. Rather, this story would be expressed with a proper "blaccent," as I am fond of calling it. Here are two quick strokes to indicate what a blaccent consists of. First, *I* is pronounced more like *ah*. So, in a blaccent *I see* is "Ah see." Probably not when someone reads the words *I see* deliberately from a page—but in rapid casual speech. Another one: *Hold on* is more like *Hode on*—again, in quick speech, not when a person is thinking about it. A person with a blaccent, saying *Hold on, now I see it*, says "Hode on, now ah see it." In many parts of the United States, we hear people with blaccents all day long every day. With the prevalence of hip-hop, blaccents are heard regularly almost everywhere in the country, as well as the world (I once heard a twentysomething in New Guinea singing precisely like Usher, right down to the black cadence).

So—by Black English we mean how most black Americans speak casually. Inner-city and working-class blacks are most likely to be able to speak a pure Black English along the lines of the Shirley story. Most other blacks can dip in and out of that repertoire to varying extents, as social parameters and subject matter require it. But it's there.

And to most Americans, it's wrong.

Perhaps warm, cool. Sexy, even. Maybe even "sharp," but then *sharp* is a word you use for someone who doesn't initially give the impression of being smart—and who you usually don't really think of as all *that* smart. Black English, we often feel, is a bad habit. A guilty *pleasure*, to be sure. But guilty.

SHIRLEY YOU JEST: IS BLACK
ENGLISH AFRICAN?

Here from underwater, Black English just looks like a different kind of English but not a lesser one: a golden retriever rather than a yellow Labrador. However, if you have ever heard a case for that that sounded, well, fishy, it may have been because the people in question live in a different lake.

Namely, some advocates for the dialect have tried an interesting argument: that Black English actually isn't even English. The idea is that Black English's differences from Standard English are based on the African languages that slaves spoke natively, with the English words as mere clothing, so to speak. Working linguists themselves have rarely espoused this idea explicitly; it is mostly put forth by people from other fields, usually education. However, many linguists have a way of genuflecting to it or letting it pass, such that it trickles into the media and elsewhere now and then.

It's the kind of idea you want to be true. At the African Burial Ground in New York, we see valuable evidence of cultural preservation in the emblem on a coffin lid being possibly the same used on funereal garments by the Akan group in Africa (who speak Twi, as it happens). We are fascinated that the basket weaving and naming patterns of the Gullah people of South Carolina are direct inheritances from African cultural practices—and even more that they sing African-language songs that they no longer understand but that Sierra Leoneans recognize as being in their Mende language. It would be really neat if Black English, so often despised, turned out to be the language of African tribespeople with English words as mere camouflage. However, if that seems a bit of a stretch or too good to be true, it is both.

It just doesn't go through. It's no accident that black Americans do not have what we would perceive as African accents. Nor is it an accident that Black English's grammatical patterns

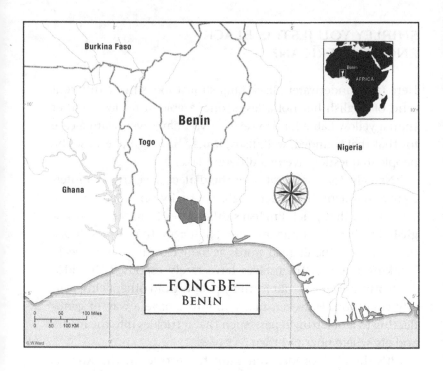

are strikingly unlike those of any language spoken in Africa (other than English!).

For example, one African language that many slaves brought to the New World was Fongbe (FAWNg-bay), another Niger-Congo language, closely related to Twi, spoken in what is today Togo and Benin. This is the language of voodoo (properly *vodun*) religion, famous from Haiti and beyond, but is also an everyday language spoken by a million and half people. Its grammatical patterns are similar to those of other languages brought to the Caribbean by plantation slaves, another of which was, again, our friend Twi.

In Fongbe, the way you render even basic sentences is quite different from anything an English speaker is used to. To say *I put the crab on the table*, you run *take* and *put* together without a word like *and*, you don't have to use articles, and you say *the table on* instead of *on the table*.

Ùn	sɔ́	àsɔ́n	ɖɔ́	távò	jí.
I	take	crab	put	table	on

Yet we would be perplexed to hear a black man in America announcing *I take crab put table on, man!*

People making the African argument imply that the connection only becomes clear with closer engagement. But in the end, they point only to a few scattered resemblances between Black English and African languages. And there are scattered resemblances between pretty much everything on earth—a screwdriver handle looks kind of like celery—and languages are no exception. You could make a beautiful case that Black English was Vietnamese on the basis of the same kind of argumentation.

The problem is clear from examining what an African language is actually like, in which case the roots of Black English in, well, English become clear. For example, just as in Black English one can leave out the *be* verb before an adjective and say *She big*, in a language like Fongbe the same kind of sentence doesn't have a *be* either. If we are talking about someone named Koku being big, as someone in Togo might, then *Koku is big* is *Kɔ̀kú klɔ́* with no *be* word.

But Black English and African languages only seem alike in this regard by accident. Black English has a general propensity for leaving *be* out—not only before adjectives but before nouns (*She a teacher*) and prepositions, too (*She in the house*). Fongbe, in contrast, does have a *be* verb that is de rigueur once you go beyond adjectives. *Koku is a teacher* is *Kɔ̀kú nyí mèsí*, never just *Kɔ̀kú mèsí*. Nothing Harlemesque about Fongbe here. In the meantime, Fongbe has no *to be* with adjectives not because it's "left out," but because what look like adjectives to us in Fongbe are actually verbs. So, *klɔ́* in Fongbe's *Koku is big* means not "big" but "bigs"—something "bigs" in Fongbe, as in many languages in the world. We don't use *be* before verbs and say that something "is walks"—and Fongbe doesn't either. As in English, in Fongbe verbs do things like get marked for tense—hence what "bigs" in Fongbe can also have "bigged." Fongbe's version of English *-ed* is to put a particle *kò* before a verb. *Kɔ̀kú kló*: Koku "bigs." *Koku kò kló*: Koku "bigged"—i.e., what English would render as *Koko was big*.

So Black English and Fongbe have no *be* before *big* for different reasons. Black English can leave *be* out all over the place. Fongbe basically uses *be* just like English except with adjectives, and then only because its adjectives are actually verbs. The dissimilarity is clear when we present the evidence. Here, *be* verbs are in bold.

Standard	Black	Fongbe
Koku **is** a teacher.	Koku a teacher.	Kɔ̀kú **nyí** mèsí.
Koku **is** on the table.	Koku on the table.	Kɔ̀kú **ɖɔ́** távò jí.
Koku **is** big.	Koku big.	Kɔ̀kú kló.

Note that Fongbe even has different *be* verbs depending on whether the sentence is about a something (*nyí*) or a somewhere (*ɖɔ́*); again, Black English is nothing like this.

Black English is more like Russian, actually, which is just as uninterested in having a *be* verb before much of anything.* Yet no one would say that Africans shaped the way people talk in St. Petersburg.

Standard	Black	Russian
Koku is a teacher.	Koku a teacher.	Kokushka učitel'.
Koku is on the table.	Koku on the table.	Kokushka na stole.
Koku is big.	Koku big.	Kokushka bol'shoj.

Black Americans are not using English words with Fongbe grammar; Black English is a grammar of its own.

In general, west African languages like Fongbe are a lot like—you may have even already noticed—Akha! Or, more familiarly,

---

* Russians: yes, Russian has a *be* verb in reserve, *est'*, but it's used for emphasis. What's key here is that sentences without it are legal, unlike in English. All languages have a way of saying *be* if absolutely necessary. Possibly most of them do *not* use *be* when it *isn't* absolutely necessary—Russian has thousands of comrades in this.

Chinese, especially Mandarin. Words are short and tend to end in vowels or *n*. Tone is used to distinguish one word from another and even for indicating tense. The syntax strikes a Westerner as rather telegraphic—articles are omissible and there is the running together of verbs in the *take-put* style. A Togolese would have an easier time with Akha or Chinese than an American, oddly enough. A black American, however, would obviously be at no particular linguistic advantage over his white neighbor if the two of them spent a year in Beijing.

Black English is nothing like Chinese—upon which the verdict on the Africanness of Black English is clear. It may well be that aspects of black intonation have some connection with the tones in African languages. But even that connection is centuries back and highly indirect—if even valid.

Where most Black English constructions come from is actually Great Britain. Remember the indentured servants we learned about in school who worked alongside slaves? Slaves in the U.S. heard a lot more English from those whites than from the owners lounging up in the house. The result was predictable, and still alive in how slaves' descendants talk in North Philadelphia, Detroit, and elsewhere.

Even when I be there with friends, I be scared—that sounds like more from Shirley, but it's actually perfectly typical Irish English. *Baby Mama* is Jamaican? People saying *my sister husband* in Yorkshire would beg to differ. *Charles, he don't hardly say nothing to her neither*—and if he were from Manchester, England, he might have been moved to tell her, *I am not never going to do nowt no more for thee*, as a real Manchester person (Mancunian, they're called, believe it or not) said. *It a letter for Shirley on the table*? Well, in Cornwall, "It's somebody at the door"—or as they would have rendered it in the grand old regional dialect there, *'Tes some wan t' the dooar*.

Even *aks* for *ask*—in Old English *ascian* alternated with *acsian*. The only question would be why *acs*—i.e., *aks*—would not be passed down to the language of the indentured servants along with *ask*. And hence, black Americans and *aks* today. The question, then, is not whether Black English is English, but what kind of English it is.

Here is where things get tricky in defending the dialect as legitimate, because so many of the differences between Black and Standard English seem, British or not, to be omissions and dilutions. Black English always seems to be about leaving things out.

WHY DOES BLACK ENGLISH TAKE A PASS?

For example, it may be interesting that Black English marks habituality more explicitly than Standard English with that *be* usage. Yet anyone might also think "But still, it's unconjugated." How legitimate *is* a dialect that doesn't have to conjugate—especially given that you can also leave off the third-person-singular -*s*? If uneducated Britishers do the same thing, we might think, then maybe they just need to get their acts together, too!

And besides, a lot of the omissions in Black English do not trace to Britain. Where Black English can just let *be* go entirely, for instance—*She my sister*—there is no dialect in England or its environs where that is legal. To put a point on it, no white dialect does that. In Black English, *Why didn't you call me* is *Why you ain't call me*, where the inversion of the subject pronoun and the auxiliary verb (*didn't you* instead of *you didn't*) is ironed out. That's a black thing, too—no Brits do that. It isn't that Black English never inverts—the same person who asked *Why you ain't call me?* could say in the next breath *Can I call you instead?* But the fact remains that he undid the inversion when the sentence started with a question word like *why*. Why?

In terms of sound, Black English also takes omission further than white nonstandard dialects. For example, all casual English clips consonant clusters here and there—to absolutely always say "Wes-*t* Side Story" instead of "Wes' Side Story" would condemn one to lonely nights. However, black speakers are more likely to say, for example, *tessin'* rather than *testing*. To grow up with

American English in all of its varieties is to be able to intuit that. For all that some are under the impression that black people have merely "Southern" accents, notice that *tessin'* sounds more "black" than "redneck," which would be *"testin'."*

So when we hear these Black English sentences—which I actually did, a week before writing this, on the New York subway—

> So what I'm supposed to do? I got to wait till she get on her feet—she my best friend.

—we certainly can't say that it has anything to do with Africa, but it's not all British either, where there is no such thing as *What I'm supposed to do?* or *She my best friend.* What's with this dialect, which so many people tell us not to look down on but so much about it seems to be *less than* what Standard English has? That is a reasonable question, and defenders of Black English step around it.*

Or—their typical observation is that Black English is, in its use of these constructions, "systematic." And it's true that Black English is not just a matter of random floutings of every rule of English grammar as speakers see fit. It's a matter of a rather compact set of practices, mostly encapsulated in the Shirley story. But the problem remains: so very many of the practices are a matter of getting a pass on doing what's required in the standard. Unconjugated *be.* In *She my best friend,* no *be* at all. *Why you ain't call me* refrains from a standard word order pattern and *baby mama* lets

---

* I myself am sidestepping something at this point: there has been a decades-long argument over whether Black English's usage of the *be* verb is modeled on that in Creole varieties like Gullah or Caribbean ones, given that slaves in South Carolina and elsewhere in the United States were often brought from West Indian plantation colonies like Barbados. I refrain from discussing that debate partly for reasons of length, partly because it has been maddeningly inconclusive, and partly because it ultimately just leads to a variation on the same question: why these black varieties of English *in general* tend so strongly to omit Standard English equipment rather than add to or substitute for it. The reason Black English does, which we are getting to, applies to Creole languages as well, the only difference being, as so often in life, degree.

go of possessive -'s. It will quite naturally seem to some that Black English may be systematic indeed: systematic *mistakes*!

After all, toy pianos are systematic, but no one records Scarlatti on them. Viruses, the Mafia, and the musical *Mamma Mia* are systematic. The systematicity argument, therefore, cannot clinch the case for Black English as legitimate, and never has. This is part of why the African argument has been attractive to some, as it escapes the inconvenience of the comparison with Standard English. But the African idea doesn't work—which leaves us right here. What's wrong with Black English?

AN AKHA IN THE ATL?

The answer requires first remembering what isn't "wrong" about it. Much of Black English is, no doubt, a subtraction of what Standard English is—but it's a pretty modest subtraction. By and large, to speak Black English is to handle the vast preponderance of what makes English difficult.

Take the irregular verbs—when's the last time you heard a black person say "thinked" instead of *thought*? Or "comed" instead of *came*? Or "paw" instead of *peed*, even? Same with the nouns—if a black person says "womans" instead of *women*, they are likely fresh off the plane from an African country and say it with a distinctly non-Ebonic accent. Nor do any black people say "childs." Black English is challengingly dissheveled in mostly the same ways as the standard dialect. An Akha, if plunked into a working-class black neighborhood in Atlanta and assigned to learn English by listening to the locals, would be just as frustrated by irregular verbs and nouns as an Akha on the same assignment in Scarsdale, New York.

Black English also includes the bulk of the things about English that are just plain subtle. *My mother-in-law is from Belgium, and that's why I'm going to learn French*, one could say in Standard English. But wait—isn't the "rule" that future tense in

English is expressed with *will*? Yet you'd be much less likely to say *My mother-in-law is from Belgium, and that's why I will learn French*. It would sound like you yourself didn't grow up speaking English. You wouldn't even say it with a more "natural" contraction: *My mother-in-law is from Belgium, and that's why I'll learn French*. It's not an utterly hideous sentence. But it only makes sense if you mean that you will pick up French passively as a result of being around your mother-in-law—"You wanna know why I'll learn French? Because my mother-in-law is Belgian, that's why, so just wait and see how I end up talking after a while." If what the sentence is supposed to mean is that because your mother-in-law is Belgian, you intend to learn French on your own, then someone saying *My mother-in-law is from Belgium, and that's why I'll learn French* would leave you tapping your ear—it's "funny" English at best. Future tense is a tricky thing in English—and it's the exact same way in Black English.

My mother-in-law is from Belgium, and that's why I'll learn French sounds not at all "Ebonic"—rather, we might expect *My mother-in-law, she from Belgium, and that's why I'm-a learn French*. Never mind the other differences, and especially never mind that *going to* is contracted to—via *gonna*, and then *gon'*—to *a*. It's still not *will* or *'ll*—Black English makes the same subtle future distinction that the standard does.

Another one: *the* is for things already mentioned—*the car I bought*—and *a* is for things introduced—*a car I want to talk about*. That's how it's taught, but it's actually hairier than this. We say *You need to buy the best car you can find*—but here, the car in question is introduced as a new topic; nobody was talking about it before and nobody can even know anything about the car yet. So why *the*? Never mind*—just note that Black English would have the same thing. Nobody on the South Side of

---

* Or if you can't help minding, definiteness is more properly about what the addressee can be assumed to know the existence of, whether or not it has actually been brought up. One knows that there exists that hypothetical best car for the person, logically, even without being able to specify anything about it, and without its having been brought up before.

Chicago would say *Man, you need to buy a best car you can find.* Black English, marking fine shades of meaning like these, is just as *ingrown* as the standard.

So Black English is chock full of the particular complexities that make English English. It's one more thing that makes the African argument so hopeless. Aware of this, we are ready for the first of two answers to the question as to what's wrong with Black English.

BLACK ENGLISH, BLACK HEBREW?

Black English's subtractions from the standard such as the absent *be* verb only run so deep. It's as if Black English underwent a close shave at some point, but only that.

And that leads us to understanding the specific nature of what's "wrong" with Black English. Black English is to Standard English is, if you think about it, what Modern Persian is to Old Persian. Or, more to the point, what Modern English is to Old English! Modern English lacks a great many of the bells and whistles—gender, *hither* versus *here*, *be* verbs versus *have* verbs, and so on—that make Old English as challenging to us to learn as German. It was Vikings who did this to English, but as adults, they couldn't learn Old English perfectly. Yet now we speak and write that rendition of Old English, understanding that no sin was committed and that the result, what we call Modern English, is not a sign of dim mental power.

Black English lacks, actually, just some of the bells and whistles of Standard English. This time, it was African slaves who were responsible, because as adults, they couldn't learn Modern English perfectly. But now black Americans speak that rendition of Modern English, and we thoroughly understand—or should, since there is no logical reason not to—that no sin was committed and that Black English is not a sign of dim mental power.

Black English is, of all things, the result of a Persian conversion on plantations of the Old South. A reasonable objection might be that if Modern English is a reduction of Old English, then for Black English to be the result of yet another pass of reduction suggests that it courts some kind of code-red linguistic breakdown. How much sanding down can a language take? you might wonder. But if there is such a thing as a dialect with dangerously inadequate grammatical machinery, then Black English offers no evidence of it. Recall that Russian leaves out *be*, too—as do countless languages worldwide. And as for subject-verb inversion, that is largely a European language peculiarity. Leave Europe, and very few languages switch the subject and the verb around in questions. What's good enough for Arabic and Chinese and Swahili and most of the languages of the world is good enough for the Ebonic among us.

YET WE CANNOT PRETEND that our social and cultural perceptions do not affect how we perceive and evaluate language. The idea that Black English is somehow illegitimate or broken can be mightily difficult to shake—even with all due understanding of the social history of its speakers. That is, one may suppose that Black English is broken language that is the heritage of a people denied education for so long—understandable, but still deformed.

Something that can help here is an odd but spot-on parallel. The difference between Black and Standard English is quite similar to that between, of all things, Modern and Biblical Hebrew!

Hebrew was enshrined on the page as the language of the Old Testament, but was no longer used as a spoken language after the second century A.D. It never precisely died, used as it was for religious, exegetical, and artistic purposes. However, it was not learned in the cradle by children; no one conversed casually in it. It was a private code, wielded by a specialist lettered caste.

Only in the late nineteenth century did Eliezer Ben-Yehuda spearhead an awesomely successful effort to bring Hebrew from

the page back into everyday life, as the language of Jews in Palestine. This meant teaching the language, fast and hard, to immigrants whose native languages were Yiddish, Polish, Russian, and
others—but mainly Yiddish. Ben-Yehuda was serious—when he
caught his wife singing a lullaby to their child in Russian he hit
the ceiling and reduced her to tears, such that little Ben-Zion
became indeed the first native Hebrew speaker in over 1,750 years
(and as such, was often lonely as a child). As soon as after World
War I, the everyday language of Jews in Palestine was Hebrew,
and a Jew caught speaking another language could be admon-
ished with *Yehudi, daber ivrit*—"Jew, speak Hebrew."

But this new Hebrew was the product of, at first, adults
learning it—to which what happened to English and Persian is
germane. What are the chances that Jews in what soon became
Israel would speak a Hebrew as complicated as Biblical Hebrew?
Based on what we have seen in this book, nil.

Modern Hebrew is certainly a complex language, as anyone
will tell you who has wrestled with its verbs, especially the
capricious future tense marking. Plus there are things like irreg-
ularly gendered nouns. If I had to learn a language fast, I'd
choose Persian over Hebrew any day. Yet in the grand scheme of
things, there is a certain "That's *it*?" quality about Modern
Hebrew just as there is about Persian. If I had to learn a language fast and the choice was between Hebrew and Russian, I'd
choose Hebrew in an instant, and there's a reason.

It's because all those adults learning Hebrew in the late
1800s and afterward shaved off some of the hard stuff. Not all
of it or even most of it—but about as much as African slaves
shaved off of English to create Black English.

Biblical Hebrew, for example, had a couple of sounds made
in the back of the throat, of the kind so prominent in its close
relative Arabic. They were what ﬠ stood for.* In the modern

---

* Hebrew letters have always looked good to eat to me for some reason. I
always want to bite them. And yes, I have bought the Hebrew letter pasta.
But it doesn't quite do the trick—they're too small. I want something like
Hebrew letter *cookies*. Or sausage.

language, few Israelis have used these sounds—as we would expect, given that the language was revived by people most of whom did not grow up using them. Modern Hebrew has a rather unusually meat-and-potatoes set of sounds for a Semitic language, and the ways they change when next to one another are less involved than they were in the Biblical version. Soundwise, Modern Hebrew seems very much to represent what would happen if a language that started out a lot like Arabic was taken up by diligent but busy grown-ups not used to gurgling when they talk.

In almost every language I know of, there is some noisome little thing that I wish, when seeing it on the page, I could just flick away like a stray cat hair. In Russian it's the soft sign ь, exerting a tricky-to-pronounce kind of disruption, viruslike, upon the sounds before it. In German, it's the irregularity of the plural marking (German toddlers sound funnier than English-speaking ones, because it's so easy to make cute plural mistakes). In Hebrew, it's the construct form I want to flick away.

To make an *A of B* construction, like the *end of the day*, the *of*-ness is expressed by a suffix on the first word. *Meal* is *arukha*, *evening* is *erev*. Meal of the evening—i.e., dinner—is *arukhat erev*. Then there's a different situation for the plural: *Son* is *ben*, *sons* is *banim*, but *sons of the covenant* is *bney ha-brit*, best known to us rendered as B'nai B'rith.

But there are countless words in Hebrew whose constructs are irregular in some way. If you want to say *evenings of* something, the plural construct form for *erev*, "evening," is *arvey* instead of *ervey* because it begins with one of a few sounds that screw things up in this way. Then lots of words that begin with those same sounds *don't* screw up, for no reason: *ever*, "side," looks and sounds pretty much like *erev* said by someone a little odd—and yet its plural construct form is just *evrey*. Then there are other exceptions that only make sense if you know arcane things about defunct distinctions between vowels that you can only see when the vowel signs are written, which in the Hebrew writing system they usually aren't. All of this is a nuisance.

What's more, with constructs the article sits funny, plunked between the words instead of sitting before them like a well-behaved article is supposed to. *The dinner* feels like it should be *ha arukhat-erev* but it's *arukhat ha-erev*.

All of this *mishegoss* surrounding the construct is the kind of thing that adult learners don't handle well, and it's no accident that it's more common in Modern Hebrew to indicate possession in a more elementary way, just saying "the A of B." So if *sgira* is *closing*, instead of saying *sgirat ha-shaar* for *the closing of the gates* (with that weird article placement, too), you can just use the word for *of*, *shel*, and say *ha sgira shel ha-shaar*. This is exactly what we would expect the founding generation of adults who adopted Hebrew as a second language to do, and they passed the habit on to today's speakers.

There are other habits in Modern Hebrew pointing in the same direction: ironing out wrinkles, corralling the weirdness into corners, or relegating it to the realm of formality. Hebrew numbers from three to ten have "backwards gender" just as they do in Arabic—and we need not even wonder whether Israelis are consistent in maintaining this oddity in colloquial speech.

One thing we know is that this is not a mere matter of things that happen naturally over time in a language for no reason. Normally—with *normal* intended as characterized in this book—i.e., Pashto, Archi—languages pile on new complicated things while they are letting other things fall apart. Normal, in Semitic terms, is Jesus's native Aramaic.

Few are aware that it is still spoken, in villages in Syria, Israel, Turkey, and Iran; I have heard it on New York streets once or twice. Time was that it was picked up by quite a few adults, when it was a lingua franca of the Near East. However, today it consists of obscure rural varieties, allowed to ingrow and dishevel for thousands of years.

And Aramaic reveals normal in all of its magnificent mess—it is, grammatically, a strikingly busier thing than Hebrew or

Arabic, even to say some of the simplest things. *He opened* is *ifθaḥ* and *it* is a suffix *-e*. When you put them together, however, it's as disruptive as the linking of two atoms is to their electron shells. Really, *ifθaḥ* plus *-e* "should" just yield *ifθaḥe*. But what you actually get is not *ifθaḥe* but *faθḥe*. Look at the difference between what "should" and what "is": the beginning *i* falls off, and the θ and the *a* trade places. It's as if instead of *Untie it* we said *Tnie-it*—and yet this is *regular* in Aramaic (a Western Aramaic dialect, for the record). In Hebrew school, in contrast, if you get this far, all you have to do to say *He opened it* is say *He opened it*: *Hu* (he) *patakh* (opened) *oto* (it).

Another distraction from the Persianesque social history of Modern Hebrew is claims, analogous to the African ones for Black English, that Modern Hebrew is another language in Hebrew skin. My e-mail buddy Ghil'ad Zuckerman treats Modern Hebrew as a Yiddish-Semitic hybrid, including a marvelous comparison of Modern Hebrew to a cuckoo's egg sneaked into another bird's nest to be raised as offspring under false pretenses (I guess the cuckoo speaks Yiddish). The *shel* possessive, for example, does happen to be the way Yiddish does it as well: e.g., *dos bux fun di studentn,* "the book of the students." Then there are expressions like *Ma nishma?* "How are you?" which translates as "What's heard?" when Yiddish's *Vos hert zikh?* translates as the same thing.

But it would be strange if a variety of Hebrew created by so many Yiddish speakers didn't have some "Yiddishe" expressions like this. When it comes to the grammar overall, though, Modern Hebrew offers not even a hint of what Yiddish is in a specific sense—i.e., a variety of German. The *shel* possessive may be like Yiddish's version, but we're back to screwdrivers and celery—it's also like the possessive in countless languages worldwide: "the A of B" is an almost inevitable way of expressing the possessive (such as in English, for one). And that is the key here. It's more fundamental—easier—than the quirks of the Biblical Hebrew construct, just as other Modern Hebrew traits are a matter of untangling rather than anything particular to Yiddish, such as easier sounds, making numbers' gender sensible, etc. The question is whether Modern Hebrew's grammar is about Yiddish specifically or about adults having made Hebrew a little easier in a general way, regardless of which language they grew up with.

What answers the question is that Modern Hebrew grammar is not, overall, Yiddish or anything close. Hebrew, with its crazy verbs where vowel changes are central, and then there are prefixes and suffixes to learn on top of that, is hard-core Semitic, presenting the same challenges as Arabic on all levels, *Ma nishma* or not.*

Modern Hebrew is slightly simplified Biblical Hebrew. Black English is slightly simplified Standard English. No one is under any impression that Modern Hebrew, despite its Persian conversion, is not valid speech. The illogic in the general evaluation of Black English as "bad grammar" is clear.

IS BLACK ENGLISH INGROWN?: A QUESTION THAT MUST BE "ASSED"

Yet despite being a product of streamlining, a close shave, Black English is human language, and as such, like all human language, it is intricate. Not just "systematic," but complicated—in ways of its own. This leads to the second answer to the question as to whether there is anything wrong with Black English. It has grammar that Standard English doesn't—but this can be devilishly hard to perceive. We're trained not to.

---

* The same verdict applies to Paul Wexler's argument that Modern Hebrew grammar is half Slavic. Russians learning Hebrew today after moving to Israel find nowhere to grab on to, and would be surprised to hear that the language they are struggling with is a version of their own with different words.

Grammar is many things. We have seen it in tones. We have seen it in particles. But who'd know, to bring this topic up just one more time, that you can also find grammar in butts?

In Black English, the word *ass* has a wide range of usages that sound, in passing, like random vulgarity, but in fact in ways make the grammar a richer one than Standard English's. *What??* I know. But take sentences like these:

My ass musta been crazy. I ain' had on no jacket.

That other woman lived with his ass twelve years.

She ain' marrying his stupid ass.

Ain' nobody tol' his ass that.

She the one sat down and ate that whole pie with her greedy ass.

All of these are sentences of Black English. Pungent, to be sure, but vulgarity does not cancel out structure. In those sentences, *ass* is used as a subject, an object, an object of a preposition, and in a double object construction (like *told him that*, but here rendered as *told his ass that*).

Note that these go beyond the more limited idiomatic uses of *ass* in mainstream English. All can say *I worked my ass off* and *Tell him to get his ass out of here*. But the list of sentences above is something else: these are *Black* English sentences. To the extent that one hears them used by younger whites these days, it is part of the mainstreaming of black speech over the past fifteen years or so, partly via the nationwide embrace of hip-hop.

There is indeed structure here. You can't substitute other words for the posterior. No one would say *That other woman lived with his buttocks twelve years*, even if technically she did, given that his buttocks came with his general person. Nor would anyone exclaim *My rear end must have been crazy!* This usage of *ass*—indeed a "usage"—is non-literal, almost a new pronoun. To speak the dialect is to know that this *ass* is not meant literally. *Your ass in trouble!* someone says—to which the proper answer could be neither *No it isn't!* or even *No it ain't!*

Generally, in terms of the above sentences, we all know that buttocks do not fall into deranged mental states, nor do they marry. And as for eating a pie with one's *derrière*, the notion only corresponds to reality in a decidedly abstract sense.*

Moreover, you can't toss this *ass* just anywhere. *Carol is a doctor ass* doesn't work—this usage of *ass* cannot be used as a predicate, to put it in linguistic terms. *Ass* here also has to refer to living things (the animate, as linguists put it)—you don't say about a car *That's when I bought its ass.* Nor can you append *ass* to someone's name—*Rosalie ass, where you at?* is not Black English or much of anything. The correct sentence, of course, would be *Rosalie, where you ass at?*

In this, Black English actually joins a great many languages of the world in having colorful non-literal uses like this of certain nouns. A few decades ago, casual French was doing it with *apple*: *C'est pour ma pomme*, literally "It's for my apple," meant *It's for me.* In Yoruba (of Nigeria) they do it with *body.* In one dialect of Mayan, there's no such thing as a straight indirect object pronoun. If you're saying something about what was given or said *to him* or *to her*, then you have to say *to his mouth*!

All of these things are ways in which those languages are neat; Black English has one, too—and as in all such cases, it's grammar, of the kind that must be "learnt." One can imagine the poor Akha in Atlanta dutifully coming up with things like *My ass am dreaming* and *The ass of Carl is in trouble*—he'd need practice. Like English, Black English is hard—but to notice it, you have to listen in a different way than we're used to.

---

* My favorite sentence from an article I used for this topic: *Do not let your dispatcher, with her non-English-speaking ass, dispatch me.* This was an actual spontaneous sentence, produced by a soldier in Iraq. And—a favorite spontaneous *ass* from a white person of my acquaintance, different from this particular Black English usage but a treasure nonetheless: *That's fine if you want to end up stuck in an ass life.* To think that a word referring to the gluteus maximus could drift into such a dazzling range of usages the way it has—someone (who is not me) should do a book on *ass* alone. It shouldn't be too long, but still. Or, even better—how about a blog?

* * *

WE HAVE SEEN, FOR EXAMPLE, how in a language little particles can carry a heavier load in getting meaning across than most of us would imagine possible. In Akha, recall, little *là* conveys that you are asking a question that you expect an affirmative answer for, while little *mía* means that what you're saying is something you know from having perceived it by ear. Cantonese Chinese is a champion in this regard, stringing particles together like a chef seasoning a dish from the spice rack.

One might have occasion to say, for example, *She got first place*. However, just intoning it in isolation would be more likely of a robot (or someone doing textbook exercises learning English as a foreign language). More realistically, you would couch that observation within a context of your opinion about the matter, assumptions about whether her taking first place was expected, and so on.

So suppose you said *And she got first place, too, you know*—a genuine human utterance, conveying that the statement is a valuable addition to the stream of conversation and that her taking first place is not as widely known as it should be. Cantonese gets these contextual aspects across not with initial *and* plus appended *too*'s and *you know*'s, but with a string of particles:

Kéuih	ló-jó daih	yāt	mìhng **tìm ge la wo**.
she	took number	one	place

The four particles here are kind of like the four basic elements of Thai cooking—fish sauce, chili, palm sugar, and lime—each contributing a facet of the general flavor. *Tìm* conveys evaluation, ranking; *ge* gives a note of assertion; *la* marks the issue as a current concern; *wo* adds that the issue is newsworthy. This is perfectly normal: if you stroll through a Chinatown where people are speaking Cantonese, they're doing this—24/7. And there are about thirty of these little buggers.

None of that seems to have much to do with how black

people talk in Newark—but only because we are trained to filter out so much of what we hear them say as "slang" rather than grammar. You will hear, for instance, *Dem trains don't be runnin on time, yo*. Note: not *Yo! Dem trains don't be runnin on time*. That *Yo!* is an interjection, and is hardly limited to black people. I mean a *yo* appended to the end of a statement, uttered on a low "tone"—thus, neither is it *Dem trains don't be runnin on time—Yo!!*

This "low yo" sounds, at first, like "an expression"—we associate it with *Yo!* and suppose in passing that for some reason the *Yo!* comes after the sentence instead of before. But while "low yo" certainly has its origins in *Yo!*, it is now something else entirely—it's a particle like the ones in Akha and Cantonese!

It is not used to summon people as *Yo!* is—people use it standing six inches away from the person they're talking to. The *yo* in *Dem trains don't be runnin on time, yo* is a strategy for making a novel observation without seeming abrupt. It is a kind of verbal WD-40, in Cantonese terms about halfway between the assertive quality of *ge* and the heraldic quality of *wo*.

Obviously the number of Black English speakers who could tell you that "low yo" is a cross between Cantonese *ge* and *wo* is infinitesimal, as is the number who could tell you what "low yo" "means"—just as Cantonese speakers are hard-pressed to explain what all of those particles "mean" and we draw a blank on why we say *the best thing you could do* rather than *a best thing you could do*. "Low yo" is used unconsciously, spontaneously, and yet consistently. It is, in a word, new *grammar*. Black English is more *ingrown* in this regard than Standard English—and ironically, it's in a way that does make Black English like Chinese!

ONE MORE, A FAVORITE OF mine for some reason. These are Black English sentences, all of which I caught on the fly:

We was sittin' up at Tony's.
Don't be sittin' up in my house askin' me where's the money.

I ain't got no food up in my house.
It was buck-naked people up in my house.

It's easy to just hear these as literal references to being *up* somewhere or something. After all, it is rather a regular facet of human experience to intermittently find oneself above something or someone. However, in the first two cases, the location referred to was not "up" in any literal sense; both domiciles were on the ground floor. In the case of the third sentence, I only overheard it used by a passing stranger, inviting the possibility that she lived in an upstairs unit. Yet it would be a little odd for a mainstream English speaker to specify the placement of their living space like this for no reason. Imagine someone who lived in a basement saying, across town from where they live, *There are two TVs down in my house*—not likely.

These first three sentences were uttered by black Americans, but the fourth was uttered by a white man who had many close black friends and was given to launching into affectionate (and deft) imitations of black speech. It was telling that he spontaneously included this usage of *up* in this case, especially since his apartment was, again, on the ground floor.

This usage of *up* is not spatial at all. We could think of it as another particle. It conveys that the speaker has an intimate relationship with the location. One would not say *I was up at the dentist's*—unless the dentist's office was uptown, in which case you would intend *up* in its literal meaning. You would not say *I was up at that man Mr. Taylor's* because in referring to him as *that man*, you show that you don't know him that well, such that his living space would not be one you thought of as a home away from home. One could give away an infidelity in Black English by unthinkingly referring to having been *up* at the apartment of someone who your partner has assumed you were only briefly acquainted with. The *up* would give away that the apartment was somewhere in which you had spent a lot of time in serious comfort.

To the extent that anyone is aware of this usage of *up*, they would most likely shrug it off as, again, "slang." But it lives on decade after decade, conveying this very specific shade of meaning. Elsewhere, similar constructions that connote location with an added shade of intimacy are treated as grammar. In Finnish, if a cup is on a table, you convey the *on*-ness with the suffix *-lla* on the *table* word: *pöydi-llä*. But if a ring is on a finger, then you convey the *on*-ness with the suffix *-ssa* on the word for *finger*: *sorme-ssa*. The *-ssa finger* suffix connotes a more intimate contact than the *cup* one, *-lla*. A ring is all over that finger and stays there. A cup is just poised on the table, with only the bottom in contact with it, and it's only there for a spell. In Korean, *put* is a different word depending on how intimate the puttage is. You *nohta* a cup on the table, *nehta* an apple into a bowl, and *kkita* a videocassette into its box.

But if in Black English you're *at* the dentist but *up* at your cousin's house, it's just "slang"? It won't do to object that this *up* doesn't make literal sense. In what sense is making *up* with someone vertical (when in certain cases it distinctly isn't!)? If someone is all washed *up*, what are they above, and in what way is someone successful more horizontal?

Once again, Black English is *ingrown* in a way that the standard happens not to be. The "*up* of intimacy" is yet another *grammatical* particle in Black English, as specifically contentful as the ones in Akha and Cantonese. Black English is, despite its randy associations, a grammar, a system—and a challenging one to make sense of, at that. It is, in a word, *intricate*.

IS SPOKEN BROKEN?

Black English, then, is more ingrown and intricate than Standard English in some ways, and to the extent that it lacks a certain degree of the complexity of the standard, this is because it underwent the same streamlining process as Old English did to become that very standard, and Hebrew did to become the language spoken today as a nation's vehicle of expression. Black

English is not "bad grammar" under any logical conception—unless we can seriously condemn our own mainstream English as crummy Anglo-Saxon.

My pointing this out is not to be taken as a call for black people to be able to skip learning Standard English. Certainly someone who could only communicate in the language of the Shirley story would be unlikely to get an upwardly mobile job, whether or not that way of speaking is "intricate." The proper idea is that many people will be bidialectal, using Black English in casual settings and the standard in formal ones—as a great many already do and always have.

This is, in itself, rather unfair and illogical. It's often said that we need a standard variety of English in order to understand one another, but really, how many Americans find the language of the Shirley story difficult to understand? We can imagine a hypothetical America in which everyone was allowed to speak and even write their home variety of English and the country would keep running. That would be harder to manage with the languages in many countries, such as Germany or Italy, or even parts of countries such as the Mandarin-speaking part of China or the Hindi-speaking part of India, because those four languages come in varieties so distinct as to challenge mutual comprehension. But that's not true of American English. There are exactly two varieties of American English that would challenge the uninitiated in any real way—Gullah Creole spoken by isolated blacks in South Carolina and Georgia, and Hawaiian "pidgin" (actually a real language like Gullah, properly classified as a creole). That involves just three states out of fifty, and few Americans beyond where these creoles are spoken ever encounter either of them. By and large, Americans can always understand one another with little effort.

The reason we find the idea of all Americans using their home dialects in public and print so bizarre, then, is not about comprehensibility, even if we convince ourselves otherwise. It's about social evaluation: Black English is read as inappropriate for the formal. And that will not change.

However, by "social evaluation" I refer only to the issue of contextual appropriateness, senseless yet still unavoidable, like fashions. I was informed somewhere along the line that to wear pants with little pleats below the waist conveyed old age, despite that aesthetically I kind of like them. I therefore conform to that, because I can't change that evaluation as silly as it is, and I must admit that as time has gone by I have internalized that evaluation of pleats myself. We are all human.

What I do not mean, however, is what most people mean when barring Black English from the formal, which is an underlying sense that it is "broken." It isn't, and ideally we would hear Black English as casual yet intricate. I might illustrate the desired frame of mind thusly.

When I hear a teenaged black girl speaking in a formal setting and unable to avoid slipping in the occasional *aks* or elided third-person -*s*, I, like anyone else, hear her as someone who would be better off being able to make a more complete switch to Standard English. Speaking the way she does—able to "fake" standard for a stretch but prone to dropping in Black English features when she gets comfortable—will leave her always sounding less than brilliant, just like wearing pleated pants would make me look something less than young. I muse that she'd have been better off with the "elocution" training that Americans (including black ones) tended to get in the old days, including contests in what was then known as oratory.

However—and this is where people get lost on this—I do not feel that the teenager has committed "grammatical errors." She has not, in any way that makes logical sense: again, Modern English is not erroneous Old English.

This means that when I heard the twentysomething woman on the train saying *So what I'm supposed to do? I got to wait till she get on her feet—she my best friend* to a (black) friend of hers in a casual conversation where Standard English was not necessary, I was enjoying, actually, how well spoken she was in her overall conversation. Yes, well spoken—she was an articulate person. She had a way of putting things; she was an intuitive artist with speech, casual though it happened to be. And not in a "quaint" way—I wasn't savoring her "folk wisdom." She was just a good talker, period.

What distracts many from feeling that way about how she was talking—including many black people—is a basic sense that her speech must be somehow lesser, inaccurate, faintly lamentable, because it isn't how English is typically written. As literates, we inhale a sense that The Language is on the page, unchanging, while what goes on in the mouth, unscribed and changing from decade to decade, is a variation on the written—and, in its impermanence and fluidity, inferior.

But to feel this way is to demote most of the language that humans worldwide use today and ever have used as doggy-mouth sloppy. Cute, with a smell you might come to love like the gamy redolence of gas stations, but still sloppy. In the next chapter we will evaluate the unexamined assumption we tend to operate under, that written language is "the real thing."

CHAPTER FOUR

LANGUAGE IS ORAL

Y ou do not speak in letters.

You speak in sounds. There's a difference, and far beyond the well-known fact that English spelling is absurd. So you know that *through* is spelled with far too many letters. In fact, in the International Phonetic Alphabet, of the kind that Henry Higgins in *Pygmalion* was using when transcribing speech, *through* has only three "letters," not seven. The system has one symbol for each sound, and English has forty-four sounds despite its mere twenty-six letters. *Through* comes out as [θru] (International Phonetic Alphabet symbols are packaged in brackets; think of them as bookends). Note that *th* is not two sounds—certainly not *t* plus *h*—but one thrust of your tongue between your teeth. *Awe* comes out as just one "letter," this one: [ɔ].

The divergence between sounds and letters goes further than this, though. (Note: *though* is six letters but just two sounds: [ðo]).

WHY LETTERS ARE FAKE

For example, when someone says *walkin'* instead of *walking*, they may be dropping a letter, but they are not dropping a sound.

They are just using a different one. To show what I mean, we need to see what that different sound is.

Say *finger* (I hereby pause as you do), and now say *singer.* Note that they do not precisely rhyme. With *finger*, you actually pronounce the letters *n* and *g*. With *singer* you do something else. You produce a consonant that English has no letter for, but the International Phonetic Alphabet does: [ŋ]. It has a name, "engma." Thus the sounds, as opposed to the letters, in *singer* are [sɪŋɹ̩], where the [ɪ] is "ih" rather than "ee" (you don't say "seenger" like Speedy Gonzales) and the dot under the *r* means that it's a growly syllable of its own without a true vowel.

In truth, even the *n* in *finger* is an engma. You don't say, if you think about it, "finn-ger." You say [fɪŋgɹ̩], using that same weird sound for *n* that's in *singer*, but then pronouncing the *g* as you don't in *singer*. You'd never know this from English letters. The Vietnamese name *Nguyen* starts with not "nnn-g" but with engma—pronounce it "Nnn-GOO-yen" and you sound dopey to the Vietnamese. You start *Nguyen* with the same sound that's in the middle of *singer*, which no English word begins with. *Nguyen* starts with [ŋ].

Now that we know engma is a real thing: engma is also the sound of *ng* in *walking.* The sound of that *ng* is not actually a sequence of *n* and *g*—it's the same sound you make in the middle of *singer*. Try it—you don't say "walkinuh-guh." You kind of swallow the *ng*—i.e., you make a nice engma. Using that *aw* symbol [ɔ] from *awe*, *walking* in the International Phonetic Alphabet is [wɔkɪŋ], and not [wɔking].

But note that this leaves at the end of *walking* not two sounds *n* and *g*, but just one, [ŋ]. And there is only one sound at the end of *walkin'*, too—a simple *n*. Which means that the difference between *walking* and *walkin'* is not a "dropped letter" *g* but an alternation between two *sounds*, [ŋ] and [n]. It's the fakery of English letters that makes us think that we are saying *ng*—more properly, [ng]—when we aren't.

The slip between letters and sounds even blinds us to the intricacy of the language we speak. One often hears stage actors making sure to always pronounce *them* as "thehm." As they should, we might think, because that's what "the word is." That's how it's spelled, after all. Yet if that's what the word "is," then why does "thehm" so often have a note of falseness? Truly, the way any native English speaker often renders *them* in rapid, casual speech—whether they drive trucks or are Rhodes Scholars—is "thum." In *I'll tell them*, you pronounce *them* as "thehm" when reading it out in an explicit fashion, school-recitation style. But the way to pronounce it in a natural way is "I'll tell thum."

Some might suppose that stage actors need to speak clearly, but "thehm" does not aid clarity in any way, if you think about it. If an actor says "thum", just what else might the audience think she means? What's a *thum*, other than a perfectly ordinary English pronoun? If someone said *It's high time I bought a thum* you'd have no idea what it meant. And *thumb* is not at issue, because of another slip between letters and sounds. *Thumb* begins with the "hard" *th* of *thick* and *thin* (linguists' [θ]), while *them*, in any rendition, starts with the soft one of *this* and *that* (linguists' [ð]). Plus, *thum* is always pronounced without an accent—*I'll TELL thum*; *thumb* almost always has an accent, which distinguishes it from *thum* as vividly as the sounds do. Maybe just now and then life squeezes you into a situation where you need to pronounce *thumb* without an accent—*Why can't you just use your own thumb?*—but let's face it, that's hardly everyday life.

Actors resist the reality of "thum" out of a basic illusion very hard for any person to shake in a literate society: that words really "are" the way they are written. That is, we tend to think we speak letters, written words. But written conventions have a way of obscuring linguistic reality. "Thehm," for example, is indeed genuine English, but it's an accented form in contrast to an equally genuine unaccented form that sounds somewhat different from the accented one. *"Thehm" we can talk about* is a normal sentence, as is *Me and "thehm" went yesterday.*

But just as often, English makes use of the unaccented form, "thum." By no means a lapse or mere static, "thum" is absolutely required of anyone who wants to speak English without sounding like a Martian or a competent but not quite acclimated newcomer to the language. But because our writing conventions "unravel" the language and transcribe both the accented and unaccented forms as *them*, the actor is distracted into supposing that always saying "thehm" is "rendering the text properly," as if speaking, which the character portrayed is supposed to be doing, is "text"—again, that illusion of speaking "letters." I have even heard actors jamming phony "thehms" into the "text" when spouting the vibrantly choppy, earthy vernacular of David Mamet plays.

When people just take down how a language's pronouns really work when it hasn't been written, then they readily cast into writing the difference between accented and unaccented pronouns. They can see that the difference is part of the language's system—i.e., its grammar—rather than seeing the unaccented pronouns as merely lazy or unclear. In Chapter One I gave one sentence of the Leti language spoken on one island in Indonesia. In that language's description, there are two sets of pronouns, the accented ones and the unaccented ones. It's clear that the unaccented ones are short versions of the accented ones. The *I* one happens to just stay the same, but because otherwise pronouns *always* come out a certain way when unaccented, they are accepted as regular, "real":

	accented	unaccented*
I	au	au
you	oa	o
he, she	ea	e
we (me and you)	ami	a
we (me and them)	ita	i
y'all	mia	mi
they	ira	i

---

* Linguists call these the *clitic* forms. Or: linguists, these are what the author analyzes as the clitic forms. Clitics are the halfway point between separate word and prefix (or suffix)—kind of stuck to the root but not completely.

In Leti translations of Tennessee Williams plays like *A Street-car Named Desire* and *A Cat on a Hot Tin Roof*, we can be pretty sure that when Stanley Kowalski or Big Daddy meant "thum" instead of "thehm," they would say *i* rather than *ira*.

If English were a hitherto unknown "coconut" language like Leti, then linguists would describe its pronouns something like this, with the unaccented pronouns that hover "under the radar" in written English in bold:

accented	subject unaccented	object unaccented
I	I	me
you	**y'**	you
he	he	**um**
she	she	**er**
we	we	us
they	they	**thum / um**

That is, on the basis of sentences like *Y'don't even know 'er*, which you can't be a native speaker of English and never say. And note that "thum" can also come out as "um," written, when it is, as *'em—Tell 'em!*

It's an odder thing than we often know, this sense that writing is what language is. If I tell you to think of a word, any word, you most likely envision a written word in your head as you conceive of it. If the word you come up with is *thumb*, for example, you don't only imagine a thumb, but accompany it with the written word *thumb*, à la *Sesame Street*. It's inevitable in a society where most people learn to read and write from a very early age and are always surrounded by text, whether they are habitual readers or not—e.g., signs, labels, words on packages, mail, headings on the television screen.

This sense of a word as a written thing, however, is an add-on as human essence goes. If you tell an illiterate person to think of a word, they will think of a thing or a concept—but not along with a written label. How could they, after all? Crucially, only two hundred out of six thousand languages are written much, which means that speakers of almost all the world's languages are quite accustomed to thinking of words as pictures in their native languages (although they readily do it in the Big Dude language they use with the outside world—but there are only so many of those).

For that reason and others, here underwater, language is analyzed as an oral phenomenon. Linguists, interested in what language as a species trait is, study speech, not writing. How people happen to write is of minor interest to linguists and irrelevant to how we gather data. I was technically cheating in asking the Persian man to write verb conjugations rather than tell them to me while I transcribed them.

To get a sense of how deeply peculiar the idea is that written language is somehow "the real thing," it helps to step away from our deeply imprinted conceptions about our own language and take a look at the "written is real" fallacy elsewhere.

THE LANGUAGE THAT ISN'T REAL

Let's try the teardrop isle, which is as deeply imprinted in my mind as *Ceylon* as Zimbabwe will always be *Rhodesia*, because I learned geography in the early seventies. Today, however, we speak of Sri Lanka. And what they speak there is not called Sri Lankan or Ceylonese.

The Indo-European language family spreads both across Europe and into Asia, encompassing, for starters, Persian, Pashto, and the Iranian brood. The Indo- part of the name refers specifically to languages of India that developed from Sanskrit, including Hindi, Urdu, Bengali, Gujarati, and others (including Nepali). They comprise the Indo-Aryan group, but the southern part of India is home to languages of quite another language family than Indo-European, called Dravidian. None of them, such as Telugu, Kannada, Malayalam, and Tamil, are exactly

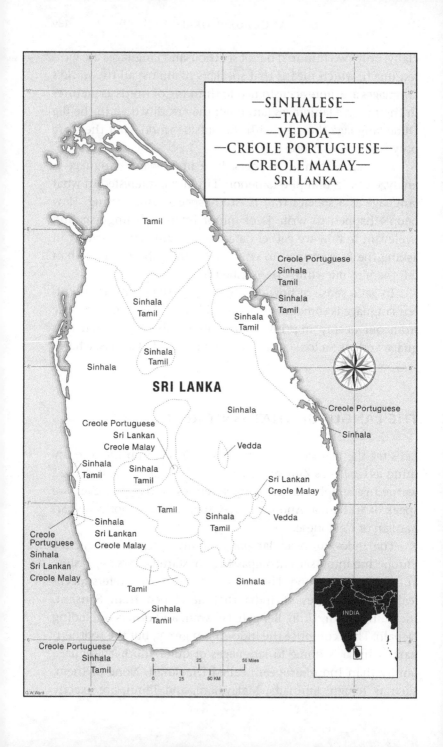

—SINHALESE—
—TAMIL—
—VEDDA—
—CREOLE PORTUGUESE—
—CREOLE MALAY—
SRI LANKA

Tamil

Creole Portuguese
Sinhala
Tamil

Sinhala
Tamil

Sinhala
Tamil

Sinhala
Tamil

Sinhala

Sinhala
Tamil

SRI LANKA

Sinhala

Creole Portuguese

Sinhala

Creole Portuguese
Sri Lankan
Creole Malay

Vedda

Sinhala
Tamil

Sri Lankan
Creole Malay

Sinhala
Tamil

Tamil

Sinhala
Tamil

Vedda

Sinhala
Sri Lankan
Creole Malay

Creole
Portuguese
Sinhala
Sri Lankan
Creole Malay

Tamil

Sinhala

Sinhala
Tamil

Creole Portuguese
Sinhala
Tamil

0   25   50 Miles
0   25   50 KM

INDIA

G. W. Ward

household names beyond where they are spoken, but they are the languages of millions.

Given that Sri Lanka lies south of India, we would expect that Dravidian would extend to it, and it does: Tamil is spoken there as well. But mostly in the northeast. Elsewhere, the main language is Sinhalese—which is another Indo-Aryan language, having skipped over the Dravidian territory.

No one knows just why the skippers felt the need to skip so far, but the skipping happened in the fifth century B.C., while up north Old Persian was still being spoken in what is today Iran. Today twelve million in Sri Lanka still speak Sinhalese daily. And what they speak is a language indeed, full of ways to express life's experiences that differ fascinatingly from what we speakers of Western European languages are used to.

Typical of Indo-Aryan languages, for instance, is a neat way of distinguishing whether something was deliberate or accidental. Sinhalese, like a good Indo-European language, has ample case endings (which is why English is a weird one), and so *miniha* is man while *miniha-tə* means "to the man," as in giving him a present. But in Sinhalese "to-ness" is also about what happens *to* you.

Vanilla to us: "The man runs," *Miniha duwənəwa.** But if the man sees something, and the something, let's say, is an elephant, which is *aliyawə* in Sinhalese, then you'd think the way to say *The man sees the elephant* would be this, where the verb "see," *peenəwa*, comes at the end because Sinhalese is that kind of language:

Miniha aliyawə peenəwa. "The man sees the elephant."

But it isn't—running and seeing are different things. Running is an action; seeing is an experience. It happens *to* you, and in Sinhalese, you have to say so. The proper sentence is:

Miniha-tə aliyawə peenəwa.

---

* The ə is a schwa, the furry little sound of *a* in *about* and *o* in *lemon*—note that despite how those words are written, we do not say "ah-bout" or "leh-mahn."

Essentially, "*To the man* was a seeing of an elephant."

This is the same frame of mind that leads to that Spanish kink with *gustar* such that you say *Me gusta comer*, "It pleases me to eat," for *I like to eat*—but in Sinhalese that perspective is applied much more widely. Using the same trick, Sinhalese can even get across the fact that while running can be deliberate and usually is, it can also be something you break into by accident on impulse. If our man runs in that way, it happens to him rather than being initiated by him, and you can say it that way by adding the "to" ending: *Miniha-ṭə diwenəwa*, "The man breaks unthinkingly into a run," in which the verb form is different by one sound *i*, too, which indicates the accidental quality of the event.

Sinhalese is overall quite ending-mad, again as we would expect of a good card-carrying Indo-European language compared to Chinese or Akha or Keo. Here are the hoops that Sinhalese can put a verb through—and this is the pattern for just one verb type of three. This is not to be "learnt" but just to be observed:

do	kərənəwa
did	kerua
do for real	kəranne
did for real	kerue
would do	kərətot
would have done	keruot
let's do	kərəmu
do it on purpose	kərannan
do it by accident	kəraawi
is allowed to do	keruaawe
to do	kərannə
doing	kərətə
done	kərəla
the act of doing	keriimə

And nouns are just as busy: *miniha* is *the* man, but *a* man is *minihek*, while *the men* is *minissu*.

You get the point: Sinhalese is ingrown, *always* marking fine shades of meaning that a language could do without (like English: Did it for real? Do it by accident? Please!!).

And yet, in real life, the fact is that what I have just shown you is thought of as *not the real language!!!!*

That is, the Sinhalese we just saw is thought of as unworthy of public discourse or the printed page, except in artful scatterings for purposes of "flavor." This Latinate marvel with enough verb forms to sink a boat is considered, of all things, unsophisticated.

And yet, it's the language that all Sinhalese speakers use in everyday life, regardless of social class or educational level. As such, it's not that people use it with their heads hung low. However, it's thought of as something only fit for talking. Sri Lankan Tamils who speak fluently the language I just presented will actually insist that they "don't speak Sinhalese." The "real" language is considered to be something else.

Namely, the real language is considered to be Literary Sinhalese, used in writing and in public language such as addresses and news broadcasts. It is, essentially, a different language from the everyday language: almost no one can speak it comfortably without writing out what they want to say beforehand. Even the most basic words can be completely different, creating pairs that feel in Sinhalese rather like English ones like *eat* and *dine*, *baby* and *infant*, *help* and *assist*, and *throw up* and *vomit*, except in such proliferation that the literary variety feels like a code rather than just a matter of starching things up a bit.

You get a sense of how arbitrary such distinctions are in English when seeing them in an unfamiliar language. Fancy Sinhalese has *asala* for *near*, while the spoken language has *gāva*; in the same way, they have *siyallama* versus *sērama* for *all*, and *kalhi* versus *koṭa* for *when*. Even the pronouns are different: *I*, *you*, and *he* are *mama*, *to*, and *hetema* on paper but *mamə*, *ohee*, and *eyaa* in conversation.

Alone, things like this would make Literary Sinhalese "different" from spoken Sinhalese rather than "realer" than it. What makes Literary Sinhalese thought of as "realer" are things that almost oddly parallel the differences between Standard and Black English. Conjugation, for one: the literary language does it Spanish-style, with endings for person and number, such that you get for the verb *go*:

mama	ya-**mi**	I go
to	ya-**hi**	you go
hetema	ya-**yi**	he goes

But in spoken Sinhalese, the verb stays the same with all pronouns:

mamə	yanəwa	I go
ohee	yanəwa	you go
eyaa	yanəwa	he goes

Shades of Black English having *the way he walk*. And wouldn't you know, there's a *be* verb issue. Spoken Sinhalese leaves it out: just as Black English would have *He a teacher*, spoken Sinhalese has *Eyaa goviyek*, "He teacher." In the written language, you have to have a *be* verb (or another marker we don't need to dwell on—the point being that there has to be something). With the verb at the end as always and with the literary form for *he*, in the "real" Sinhalese *He is a teacher* is:

Hetema	goviyek	**veyi**.
he	teacher	is

"He is a teacher."

Yet as we saw, spoken Sinhalese is overall an *intricate* language. It takes it a little lighter than the written language, which is more ingrown, with its separate present-tense verb suffixes for *I*, *you*, and *he* (and *we*, *y'all*, and *they*, too; I didn't show those) and having to actually have a bit of stuff to show that something *is* something else, when putting the two some-things next to one another gets the relationship across just as well. Surely this is due to the fact that over the millennia, Sinhalese has been learned by an awful lot of Tamil speakers—the Persian conversion as always. The island is small; new speech habits could always become general pretty quickly (as they likely did on Flores in Indonesia as we saw in the first chapter).

The literary language, in the meantime, was something preserved in amber in documents tracing as far back as the 800s A.D., carefully preserved apart from the changes that had created the spoken language. Only in the 1700s was Literary Sinhalese resurrected and imposed as the formal language, to be taught in schools and used in the public forum despite the gulf between it and the language as it was actually spoken by then. Cultural pride motivated that decision, in the wake of colonial domination by the Portuguese and Dutch, and so be it. Yet the idea it conditioned, that the way Sinhalese was spoken by then was "not real," was no more logical, it must be admit-ted, than a decision would be that the English of *The New York Times* is "unreal" and that heretofore Paul Krugman ought to write in Old English.

WRITING: A LATECOMER TO THE BALL

The idea of an antique rendition of one's language via scratches on paper as more authentic than how one speaks it in the here and now is a very modern condition. Language is at least 80,000 years old, as this is the age of the first evidence of an artistic sensibility in humans suggesting the possible development of linguistic ability.* Language may very well trace further back to the origin of the species, 150,000 years ago (as I highly suspect, despite the curiously visceral appeal many seem to find in language having "multiple origins"). Writing, however, began only 5,500 years ago, in Mesopotamia, and widespread, cross-class literacy was rare among any humans until just a few centuries ago.

That means that for the vast bulk of human history, people have not thought of words as writing—and certainly did not think of words in writing as somehow "better" than words they uttered. As to how peculiarly modern such a frame of mind is, dance is a useful analogy. There are systems available to transcribe ballets on paper for future dancers to use for re-creations. Yet none would think of these transcriptions, despite their usefulness, tidiness, and accessibility, as "the ballet" itself. We spontaneously understand that the transcription, no matter how good, cannot capture the fullness of dance as an experience, and alone is no substitute for a performance. The transcription, if never translated into execution, to us is a dead thing, a studious approximation, a footnote—*un*real.

One might object that the analogy slips here because casual speech is spontaneous in a way that ballet in its planned formality is not. Note, however, that the analogy holds with the dance equivalent to speech, casual "shake your [whatever; I said I wouldn't go here again in the book, so . . .]" dancing, of the clubbing/wedding sort. One could transcribe that, too—but no one would prefer reading the transcription and imagining the dancer to watching—or being—the dancer.

Or, highly trained musicians can read a musical score fluently enough to hear the music in their heads. This is partly a

---

* Claims from not so long ago that human creativity exploded with a "big bang" just 35,000 years ago in Europe and that language must have emerged then are now obsolete. This is a highly convenient obsolescence. Under the old idea, a question always loomed. By 35,000 years ago humans had occupied Asia, Africa, New Guinea, and Australia as well. How did all of them become cognitively modern if the "big bang" only happened on the European peninsula?

matter of talent but largely one of training and practice. One can imagine a society in which children were trained rigorously from an early age how to do this; some would end up better at it than others, but then this is also true of reading. In this society, all people could look at the score of a piano sonata they had never heard, or even something scored for multiple instruments, and imagine it in full in their heads.

If in this society, it came to be that people thought of written scores, in their immutable accuracy, as "music" itself and musical performance as merely taking a crack at something never truly achieved outside of print, we would find it odd. Yet this is not that far from the literate person's enshrinement of writing as language in its true form and speech as an also-ran approximation of it, most valued to the extent that it seeks to resemble writing. Think of, for instance, the reinsertion of *c* into Middle English's *parfit* for *perfect*, or the retention of the *t* in *often*, or the guilty grab-on-to-the-legs clinging to *whom*.

Writing, however, is so pervasive in our experience that it's easy for us moderns to slide into this idea that it is, in its permanence and orderliness, what language either is or at least should be. And even if our society's rendition of this does not take us to the Sri Lankan–style extreme of thinking of the language of Shakespeare as "real" and our own as humble and irrelevant, we all operate under the sense of writing as lending language some kind of reality that it otherwise lacks.

This perspective can even cast big languages like English as the lesser ones, rather than the smaller ones. In 2010, the last speaker of a tiny language of the Andaman Islands (due northeast of Sri Lanka, as a matter of fact) died. The newswires reported Bo's death, along the lines of an increasing commitment in the media to broadcasting the alarmingly rapid rate at which languages are dying today, sometimes barely recorded. This in itself was good, but then, amid the coverage a line got around that Bo was one of the world's "most ancient languages."

But how so? Written documentation of Bo of any kind barely existed, and certainly not in documents tracing back

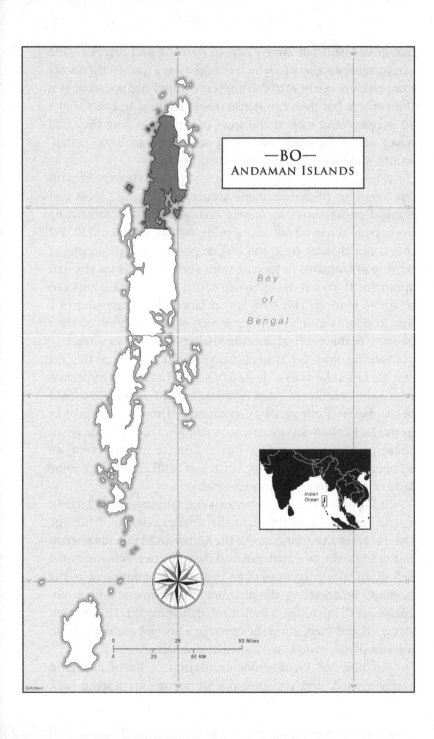

—BO—
ANDAMAN ISLANDS

Bay
of
Bengal

Indian
Ocean

| 0 | | 25 | | 50 Miles |
| 0 | 25 | | 50 KM | |

G.W.Ward

thousands or even hundreds of years. And if Bo was more ancient than, say, English, then at what point did English "begin" after Bo did? To be sure, our first written documentation of English dates only to the 400s A.D.—but that isn't when the language emerged. We know from comparing English with its Germanic relatives, those relatives' earliest written documentation, and then correlating all of this with archaeological data, that English existed as Proto-Germanic about twenty-five hundred years ago, and before this as Proto-Indo-European, and before this as . . . Well, the signal gets weak before that, but we know that it was some language spoken in Asia.

Crucially, English traces back through all of these ancestral varieties with no break, presumably step by step all the way back to the first language ever spoken, in Africa. All languages trace back to that one without a break. We have no reason to suppose that there was any point at which a group of humans, either mysteriously mute or finding themselves pathologically creative via chewing on a leaf or fungus, created some new "tongue" out of whole cloth which became English.

Of course, English only came to be *called* English at some point before 400 A.D., after Proto-Germanic had split into several languages of which English would become one. Bo was probably *called* something like "Bo" for much longer than that. English speakers were an offshoot group of Germanic-speaking peoples who migrated to the shores of the North Sea just some thousands of years ago, while the Bo people had occupied their homeland for sixty-five thousand years after a founding migration of *Homo sapiens* out of Africa.*

---

* Even here, though, we have to assume that because language always changes, and that includes sounds, what was pronounced "Bo" was pronounced in some other way five thousand years ago, and certainly some vastly other way sixty-five thousand years ago. Just keep in mind that what is pronounced "bo" in French today—spelled in writing as *beau*— was *bellus* in French's progenitor Latin, and that *bellus* came from what was *deu* in Latin's progenitor Proto-Indo-European. We'll likely never know just what *deu* came from but can be sure that it was quite different, as also was whatever that *deu* progenitor came from. The Bo language may

Surely, however, this issue of labeling is not what we think of as qualifying Bo as "more ancient" than English. If there were a head-to-head dispute over the issue between the languages' speakers, if the Bo had said, "Well . . . we've been *calling* our language 'Bo' for longer than you've been calling yours 'English,' and so . . . so . . . ," we wouldn't consider it exactly a smackdown point.

The reporters called Bo "ancient" out of a tacit sense that a written language is only as old as its documentation. Under that analysis, English "starts" with a sentence engraved onto a gold medallion in the fifth century A.D. but didn't "exist" before that—in light of which Bo, unwritten and thus leaving no earliest document to be thought of as marking its debut into "reality," seems almost imponderably antique. But would we assume that the Bo's dance traditions began only when some missionary described them in the 1800s? Or even when the Bo themselves, if they had had writing, committed a description of the dances to paper centuries earlier?

Here we see a fetishization of written language remarkable yet in the end less stark than cases like the one in Sri Lanka. However, there are cases of an even more explicit edict that Spoken is just Broken than the one in Sri Lanka. A striking example is Indonesia, where spoken reality is vastly different from what almost any print source indicates, except ones known only to a small subcommunity of linguists and fellow travelers.

THE LANGUAGE SO UNREAL THAT YOU UNLEARN IT

Indonesian is a strangely user-friendly language, as languages go. There's no gender to worry about, and no tables of case markers

---

well have once been called something like *Dʰe'pukh* (Gesundheit!). Maybe it was even called Gesundheit.

on the nouns or conjugational endings on the verbs. It has numeral classifiers, but not too many. No tones, either. You keep waiting to stub your toe on something, but in the end there is basically just one hard thing, of the kind that makes me want to flick it away.

Verbs can take one of two prefixes, whose function is to shine a little light on whether the actor or the acted-upon has the juice in the sentence. The prefix *men-* shines the little light back on the actor:

Ali **me**mukul Zainal. "Ali hit Zainal."

That one is all about what Ali did. The *di-* prefix shines that little light on the acted-upon: in this sentence what's in focus is what happened to Zainal:

Zainal **di**-pukul Ali. "Zainal was hit by Ali."

There are two annoying things going on here. For one thing, the *men-* prefix gets squashed around in all kinds of ways depending on what sound it comes before. *Hit* is *pukul*, as it is in the *di-* sentence. But when *men-* comes before it, its *n* and the *p* in *pukul* come together and become an *m*. Thus the *memukul* above instead of *men-pukul*.

Then, you might think that we could just call *di-* a passive marker, but it isn't. I gave the translation "Zainal was hit by Ali," but *Zainal di-pukul Ali* doesn't have to mean something that starkly different from "Ali hit Zainal." It could also mean, and in normal speech just as often means, something more like what we would mean if Ali had already hit various boys, with Zainal as just the latest one, and when someone asked what happened today, you said *Oh, Ali hit Zainal today*, with Zainal lightly accented.

Thus I said that *di-* shines a *little* light on the acted-upon. To learn to speak Indonesian is to learn that *di-* is not simply a passive marker, and that you have to develop a sense of a "passive lite" that also means using *di-*, of a kind that English doesn't mark with a prefix, suffix, or change in word order.

Linguists squabble over the details about *men-* and *di-*; it's a subtle business. And in a country that's home to hundreds of languages, where Indonesian is used much more as a second language than as a first, it's not hard to imagine what would be the first thing to fall away in how Indonesian is actually spoken.

As such, here's a garden-variety sentence in the standard language—i.e., what is used in schools and newspapers and what a foreigner is taught:

Anda	**men**-cari	buku	yang	sudah	**di**-baca	Ali.
you	search	book	that	"-ed"	read	Ali

"You're looking for the book that Ali read."

Both the *men-* and the *di-* prefixes are used. The *men-* gives a little shout-out to the subject *you*, as in roughly *Oh, you're the one who. . . .* The *di-* tips its hat to the object, namely the book. The word order also gets a little tricky with relative clauses like *that Ali read*—*Ali* has to go on the end.

This is not, however, the way almost any normal person throughout Indonesia would express themselves in everyday speech. For all that this kind of Indonesian thrives in print and in the media throughout the enormous nation that Indonesia is, a sentence like this one is an idealization. In Jakarta, for example, what someone would actually say for "You're looking for the book that Ali read" is not

Anda	**men**-cari	buku	yang	sudah	**di**-baca	Ali.
you	search	book	that	"-ed"	read	Ali

but

Lu	cari	buku	yang	Ali	udah	baca?
you	look	book	that	Ali	PAST	read

The main difference is no *men-* and no *di-*. Here, just *cari* and *baca* instead of *men-cari* and *di-baca*. In Jakarta, these prefixes are optional (*very* optional), but there are parts of Indonesia, such as Papua, where many people essentially never use these prefixes at all. It's quite clear where the subjects and objects are in the sentence; in the spoken language there is no "intricate" quest to be maximally explicit about it. Then, *Ali* is in the more predictable place here, before the verb instead of after it. *Lu* for *you*, for the record, comes from the Hokkien language of Chinese immigrants to Java (Hokkien is a variety of what is most often heard of in America as Taiwanese).

To learn to actually function in Indonesian is, to a larger extent than in most languages, a matter of unlearning, getting a feel for the extent to which the bells and whistles of the written language are not only unnecessary in casual speech but even rather ridiculous. As you might expect, it's the same thing with the classifiers. The standard way to say *three mangoes* is to use the proper classifier *biji*: *tiga biji mangga*. But in casual speech, more likely you'll just hear *tiga mangga*.

But here's the rub: casual Indonesian is barely acknowledged as language at all. It's something beyond even the Sinhalese situation. Colloquial Sinhalese has low status, but all are aware of it as something that stands alongside Literary Sinhalese. Literary Sinhalese, despite being seen as "realer," is also processed as a task few completely succeed in. Colloquial Indonesian, however, is thought of solely as "slang," as dismissively as Black English is in the United States, with no notion that it is worthy of extended address. In each Indonesian locale there is a different flavor of this colloquial variety, although only now are more than a few of them even being described in print, due to how deeply set the feeling is that the spoken varieties are "not real."

Even among linguists and scholars of the region, the idea that varieties like Jakarta's colloquial Indonesian are alternates to the standard language rather than just "slangy" perversions thereof, is only gradually dawning of late, if at all. As I write, online you can find ample description of colloquial Sinhalese complete with a capital C and S, whereas colloquial Indonesian occasions mostly just parenthetical mentions as "slang."

Under conditions such as those, it is unsurprising that ordinary people are perplexed or amused to see the way the language is actually spoken when committed to paper or a blackboard. It can be exceedingly difficult to get a black American who uses Black English as their daily casual speech to speak it in a real way on command, or even recognize some of its constructions on the page as things they say, such as *It's* for *There's* or *Billy book* for *Billy's book*, because of the stigma attached to it. Things are exactly the same with colloquial Indonesian. Asked to utter a colloquial Indonesian sentence or to judge one that they utter, the speaker thinks only of Standard Indonesian as "language" and their actual everyday speech as a quiet little joke, to the extent that they are aware of how much they speak that way at all.

Yet this is the way just about anyone speaks the language. The illusion that Black English is "corrupted" comes in part from the fact that it is spoken by a subgroup within society with a history of subjugated status. Colloquial Indonesian, however, is not indexed to social status or ethnicity: it's the way the language is spoken, period, by people from all walks. Among Western people who have learned Indonesian and function among its people, conversation about the language centers to a degree I have never experienced on how much you can *not* do what the books depict as how the language works.

But is this really a mere matter of something as recreational and eternally evanescent as "slang"? Could it really be that 200 million people are merely popping off with "slang" and committing "grammatical errors" all day every day? Where else do we find such a thing? Is this a *cultural* trait?

One must be open to all explanations, but clearly a less bizarre one beckons here. One is the eternal analogy with Modern English. Colloquial Indonesian exists because so many people have picked up the language as a second one and simplified its structure, as Vikings did with Old English. Standard Indonesian, today, is a taxidermal artifice in the same vein as Literary Sinhalese. *Indonesian* is the twentieth-century name for what used to be titled Malay, which now mainly refers only to dialects of Indonesian spoken in Malaysia. The earliest documented form of what we know as Indonesian, then, is Classical Malay, which was the language of the ancient courts of Johor at the tip of Malaysia and islands nearby. This grand old variety, preserved in writing and the vehicle of literature, naturally seemed a handy model for the fashioning of a new Standard Indonesian, even though it was as distant from modern speech as Shakespeare's English is from the modern language.

That's done, but it puts a big question mark over the idea that casual speech across Indonesia is "bad." To tar all of this living Indonesian as wrong means also tossing out the window not only English but all of the spoken varieties of Arabic as well as Mandarin Chinese, Swahili, and Persian.

However, we can go even further with Indonesian and the idea that Spoken is Broken. Remember the two Sulawesi languages from Chapter One, Muna and Tukang Besi? They are both relatives of Indonesian. Muna was the one with six gradations of distance, compared to Indonesian making do with just the first two:

ini "this here"
itu "that there"
maitu "that near him"
watu "that over there by him"
tatu "that up there"
nagha "that which we can hear but not see"

Tukang Besi was the language that invaders likely brought to Flores, but it is also much more "ingrown" than Indonesian. I gave one sentence of it as

| **No-** | **to-** | **pa** | ala- | **mo** | na iai-su | te kau. |
| he, | really-was-made-fetch | "-ed" | younger | sibling-my wood |

"My younger sibling was made to fetch some wood."

The point here is that it piles prefixes and suffixes on to an extent foreign to its relative Indonesian. I gave quick-sketch translations of the little bits in Chapter One, but here, look at what they actually mean:

no   third person singular plus "for real" (as opposed to hypothetically, which would be a different prefix)

to   passive

pa   make to do something

mo   in the past at one discrete time

All that on one little verb, whereas Indonesian just has its *Zainal di-pukul Ali*. Indonesian mostly leaves to context a great deal of what those Tukang Besi prefixes and suffixes mean. Presumably Ali hit Zainal for real and at one discrete time, but you don't have to genuflectively specify that when uttering an Indonesian sentence.

Indonesian compares like this to almost all of its relatives, in most aspects of grammar, and it's a tip-off to its history, of a kind we have seen throughout this book. Overall, it's not an accident that I mentioned at the outset of this section that even Standard Indonesian is strangely easy. If a language is strangely easy, then it's a sign something irregular happened to it, because ordinarily, after tens of millennia of developing private "inside jokes," as it were, languages are anything but easy.

Even when Indonesian was still Malay, it had been used as a language of trade and conquest in its region for possibly as long as two millennia. It really got around. Just as we can't be sure why Sinhalese's founders moved down to Sri Lanka, we are equally baffled, not to mention astounded, that speakers of a language of the family Indonesian belongs to, Austronesian, migrated all the way across the Indian Ocean to Madagascar!

Yet they must have, because Malagasy is not an African language as we would expect, but an Austronesian one. It includes words from, of all things, Malay, despite the fact that Malagasy's founders sailed from Borneo, where a language is still spoken that is the obvious predecessor to Malagasy but is definitely not Malay. This means that Malay speakers had imprinted their language that far to the east of Malaysia by the 300s A.D., the date that archaeology shows us. Plus, for the Malay words to be that deeply embedded in this language of Borneo (one of many, called Ngaju, for the record) by then means that the Malay had been in Borneo for centuries before.

Then from the 680s on, we have concrete evidence of a Malay empire extending to Sumatra, Java, and beyond. All of this meant countless adults learning the language generation after generation, and this is the only possible reason that today, even the Standard Indonesian of the teaching books seems almost designed to be learnable—because in a way, it was. To a Malay speaker of twenty-five hundred years ago, before Malay was imposed on so many foreigners, even today's Standard Indonesian would have seemed crude, unreal indeed—as we know from how complicated all of Malay's relatives are that never happened to be taken up by more foreigners than native speakers. "Why do you have so few classifiers?" the early Malays would have asked. "How can you drop all the prefixes and leave so much out? Where's your word for *way over there*? Why don't you have separate sets of subject and object and accented pronouns? What kind of Austronesian language is this?"

They probably wouldn't have asked that last one, but still. The Standard Indonesian today held up as the real language, while the colloquial varieties are dismissed as "slang," emerged itself as the "slang" version of a more complex ancestor. The Indonesian of casual life is the result of a Persian conversion, but then so is the standard! Which means that the casual Indonesian varieties are what happens when you get a Persian conversion twice over, just as with Black English.

A MODEST PROPOSAL: AN UNREAL
LANGUAGE AS THE UNIVERSAL LANGUAGE?

And the fact that they are dismissed rather than embraced is, in its way, sad. Because Standard Indonesian is already so approach-able, when it has undergone yet another streamlining it is one of the smoothest rides on earth.

So few languages are, and despite my revelling in their com-plexities in this book, the fact remains that the difficulty of lan-guages is a major snag in human affairs. We like to think of languages as just having different words for things, but we also know that in reality, you could memorize every single word in a language and still be a perfect linguistic idiot compared to a six-year-old native speaker who controls the grammar that puts the words together. The complexity of languages, a random, innocent result of endless morphing over millennia—ingrowing, dissheveling, and drift into intricacy—puts boundaries between people and peoples. It leads to wasted time, blind alleys, wheels spinning.

Language learning is tough. There is a report of how speak-ers of Abau, a small language of Papua, teach nonspeakers their language. They give a few basic words, and otherwise teach whole sentences, like *Give me some tobacco, I have no fire*, and *What village are you from?* Illiterate and unfamiliar with lan-guage broken down scientifically on the page, they do not teach which prefixes and suffixes mean what. Obviously, no one could actually learn to speak a language in any real way via this method. But then, languages like Abau, almost never actually learned by people past childhood, are often so complicated that the actual mechanics of the language would present the learner with a Herculean task in any case.

The miracle with colloquial Indonesian is that you practi-cally *could* teach someone the language in the Abau way. I learned this during a week in Papua, the western half of the island of New Guinea, known until 2002 as Irian Jaya (confusingly, the eastern half of the island is called Papua New Guinea). Papua, although this is little known worldwide, is part of Indonesia, such that the language all people speak other than their native ones is not Portuguese, Dutch, or English, but Indonesian. More properly, they speak a colloquial version of it, of the kind that eschews what is complicated in the standard.

It was the only place I have ever been where I could not take advantage of the fact that, where an American is likely to travel, most people speak English or, if not that, then French or Spanish. What they speak in Papua other than the obscure indigenous languages they learn on Mommy's knee is Indonesian. English is something some learn in college if they are so inclined. Even public servants often know only just enough English to manage elementary exchanges.

So—even for a one-week stay, it became clear to me that if I was going to be able to operate as a human being rather than as a squinting mute, I would have to speak some Indonesian, of which I knew precisely none when I got off the plane. I did have a handy little phrase book with a word list at the end (Lonely Planet's—highly recommended), and because I was at a linguistics conference, I had Anglophones with decades' experience in the region to consult. I got to work from the second I hit the hotel (where few of the employees could even really be said to speak English). And the glorious thing was that there wasn't much work involved.

Because Indonesian as it is actually spoken is the result of the Persian conversion twice over, learning to communicate was thrillingly close to just, of all things, learning words and stringing them together. The contrast with my week in St. Petersburg back in the nineties was instructive. My Russian was rudimentary, to put it kindly, and my attempts to get anything done were always tragically comic, to put a Chekhovian spin on it. I wanted one cup of tea with no sugar for a friend and one cup with sugar for me, and walked into a cafe to try to order that. But just that simple thing meant dealing with Russian's case markers. Using the word for *sugar* alone, *saxar*, was like sitting down in the woodwind section of an orchestra with a kazoo. To say *without sugar* means using the genitive—*bez saxara*—but *with sugar* requires the instrumenal—*c saxarom*. I barely knew this and, apprised of it by my bemused friend, could barely render it live when facing real Russians who didn't speak English and, at that time, were not much accustomed to foreigners stumbling in and butchering the language. And to this day I don't know why when I asked for an apricot, seeing legions of them hanging from a stand, I was dutifully given a steaming cup of coffee. (*Abrikosy* . . . did the *kosy* part sound like "kofi" . . . ?).

None of that in Papua—the kazoo was quite enough for a week. All I had to do was memorize some key words. Not the kind of vocabulary that language textbooks routinely present as "basic," mind you. Occasions never arose for me to engage in discussions about mothers, cousins, forks, spoons, yesterday, tomorrow, whether anything was good or bad (even there, *okay* is understood and that will do), whether or not it was raining, or what color anything was ("No, I want that *yellow* food!").

I found *want, need, buy, not, may, go, I, you, eat, drink, here, there, up, down, thank you, please, what, just a second* (so I could look in my phrase book), the numbers from one to ten, and *I don't speak Indonesian* most helpful (but if you get too confident in saying that last one, they assume you're lying and keep talking, so say it slowly with a dutiful look of slight alarm).

With those words plus a few others I no longer recall—well, okay, one of them was the word for water, which is, go figure, *air*—after just two days I was, as they say, "getting around." I had a whole weird exchange with a hotel waiter who insisted on taking my picture after bringing a cup of coffee to my room, using the above words plus one I had to ask someone the meaning of later. It turned out to mean *souvenir book*, which explained why he had considered it so important to keep telling me that I look like Barack Obama. I know—I don't in any real way, but in Papua, apparently I was the person who looked most like him who they ever saw in real life. One woman actually came up to me and touched my face and exclaimed—*anda* means *you*—

Anda, Obama! (and then some other things, but I didn't understand them).

I'll take it where I can get it. But overall, it was a joy to be able to be somewhere for so little time and actually have conversations, no matter how elementary. My final experience was one familiar to many of us—I had a bottle of *air* (i.e., water) in my bag as I went through security in Jakarta on my way to Hong Kong. The screener stopped the machine and after a few beats I said, *What?*—a word I knew. He said, *Air.* I said, *Saya minta minum di sini?* Those were the words for *I, may, drink,* and *here,* and I didn't need a stitch of case marking or conjugation or disshevelment to put them together. Wangling even that simple sentence in French, Spanish, German, Russian, Arabic, Hebrew, Navajo, Tukang Besi, Leti, Mandarin Chinese, Akha, or even colloquial Sinhalese would have required extensive tutelage beforehand, far beyond just learning some words (remember, in Chinese and Akha, despite the lack of endings, you have to do the tones). But in colloquial Indonesian the security guy understood me perfectly and said okay. I drank gratefully.

All of this was possible because of the blessings of a thoroughly oral kind of language, never committed to the page, and thought of as "not real Indonesian" by the people who speak it their whole lives long. Yet the ease of learning it made Esperanto, with its European-inspired suffixes for tense that make it hardly a plausible "universal" language for Chinese or even Indonesian speakers, seem like a parochial stunt.

To say *May I drink it here?* in Esperanto would mean pushing out *Ĉu mi povus trinki ĝi ĉi tie?* The *-us* ending is the conditional, as in *could I* rather than *can I.* In asking if it's allowed that I drink the water, I indicate that I regard the action as hypothetical. But in colloquial Indonesian people make equivalent requests 24/7 without having to indicate that they know the future hasn't happened yet. *Ĉu* is a particle that you use when asking a question—but only the kind of question that solicits yes or no, as opposed to *What do you want?* which solicits the identification of a thing. Esperanto requires that you distinguish

the two kinds of question, which only seemed necessary to Esperanto's inventor, Ludwig Zamenhof, because he grew up speaking Russian, whose *li* works the same way. And even having to
say *drink it, trinki ĝi,* is superfluous. In colloquial Indonesian you
don't have to specify that you want to drink "it." For instance,
given the context at security, there was no question as to what
"it" I wanted to drink. *Drink—minum—*alone was fine. What else
would I have wanted to drink, my iPod?

The Indonesian dismissed as "slang" is actually a human
language that does without most of what is decorative but
unnecessary in how we express ourselves in "normal" languages. It would be an ideal universal language, which all
humans regardless of linguistic background would find rela-
tively easy to learn and use. I can think of few more resonant
demonstrations of how contingent, illogical, and even destructive is the illusion that written language is "real" while spoken
language is lively but dismissable.

TALK-WRITING: PROBLEM OR PROGRESS?

This finally allows us to address an often-asked question more
productively than is usually the case when it comes up. You
may have even guessed it coming: what is the Internet doing to
language?

Here, we must first specify what is meant by language.
Clearly, we don't mean speech. No one is walking around speaking Internet or emailese. A handy thought experiment demon-
strates this. Imagine someone brought from 1985 to today.
Would they notice people speaking differently in a way that
could be traced to the Internet or e-mail? Of course not.

So the question *What is the Internet doing to language?* is very
specific. It refers to written language, and in being couched as
about "language" alone, reveals that tacit sense that writing is
what language really is.

In any case, there seem to be two fears.

One is that because people write e-mails in sloppier fashion than they once wrote letters, they will soon be unable to write in correct fashion in more formal settings. Here, we might take heart in something easy to miss in America. It is a human norm to speak more than one language, or at least more than one dialect of a language. As such there is no reason to assume that people are unable to write in two styles as well. Is it really such a counterintuitive feat of intellect to be inattendant to punctuation and spelling in e-mails but to also be able to compose a coherent memo?

After all, people do it all the time. I'm a writer, and therefore correspond constantly with other ones. Quite a few of them write e-mails exactly the way we are taught to fear, and not all of them are young, for the record. Yet you'd never know it from their published work—including before it's been copyedited. I would also be hard-pressed to say that these people are uniquely gifted at switch-hitting, nor are more than a few blessed with top-flight educations.

In any case, there is, at this point, a generation of young adults who grew up online. Who among us can say that the sum of their compositional abilities when called upon to use them is significantly weaker than that of the same cohort twenty years ago? To the extent that the sum in question among today's twenty-year-olds may be lower than we might like, the question is how different it is from the same cohort a generation ago—and note that this means not 1972, but 1990.

Upon which we recollect that in 1990, the alarm was being sounded just as loudly about the dismaying writing skills of young people—who had not grown up with e-mail. Moreover, the famous *A Nation at Risk* report decrying fallen standards in America's schools, which included the same appalled assessments of students' writing ability, dated back to 1983. Certainly reading and writing skills are not what they once were, and the reasons certainly include the declining quality of public schools and also the fact that people read ever less. But the case that the

Internet is a significant factor in this is weak. It's valid to question whether the raggediness of e-mail is a threat to the ability to write more gracefully in other contexts. However, it's important to be open to the possibility that it isn't.

A piece of data possibly relevant: in 2009, the National Assessment of Education Performance found two-thirds of American eighth graders reading at or above basic proficiency, and this figure has changed little since 1992. This suggests that the Internet has not caused such a thorough disengagement from prepared text as to dissolve the nation's ability to compose actual sentences.

The second fear would appear to be that there is just something wrong with the sheer fact of the looser, more informal style of writing in e-mail, chat rooms, blogs, Twitter, and Facebook, regardless of whether it affects formal writing. The language is, under this frame of reference, being abused, and the current permissiveness just can't be allowed.

But that discomfort is based on an assumption that what is cast into writing must be in formal style—an assumption that follows from no logical principle. Rather, until recently most prose happens to have been cast in a formal style, as a legacy from the more formal mores of a bygone era (something I wrote about in my book *Doing Our Own Thing*). Because until rather recently this was almost the only kind of prose Americans experienced or were taught, a sense set in that formality is the only "real" way to express oneself in writing. That sentiment continues to set the terms of the debate over the Internet and language.

Certainly common consensus points with approval to writers who season their prose with artfully colloquial turns here and there. Much of the writing in *The New Yorker* is of this type. But to simply write the way one talks, period, is viewed as somewhat *primitif*.

But what, precisely, is the danger in a new sphere of talk-writing? Why, precisely, is it ominous when people compose text that sounds like the way they talk rather than like the prose of *The Economist*? This discomfort with comfortable writing is reminiscent of how speakers of Sinhalese and Indonesian are taught to feel about writing in their home languages, i.e., their linguistic comfort zones.

We need not pretend that talk-writing is not altering the flavor of formal prose to a certain extent, although we are nowhere near *The Wall Street Journal* and history tomes being written in the jagged, come-as-you-are style of people's recreational contributions to blogs' comment sections. Yet again, the process began long before the Internet, as an outgrowth of the new informality culture-wide in the wake of the sixties. And in any case, let's suppose that this process does go to some degree even further as people who grew up writing online like they talk become adults. It very well may happen, although I see no reason to suppose it would be to a cartoonish extent.

The task is to identify just why a written-spoken hybrid— and again, not the "artful" kind of Calvin Trillin and David Sedaris, but writing pervaded by talking style to a much starker extent—is such a blight, and why it would be more of one for the spoken to pervade the written even more. In so many ways, we celebrate hybridity, diversity, "synergy," and, more particularly, democracy and attending to multiple voices. It would seem that a natural part of this is a larger space for the demotic in our formal prose style. One would expect a commitment to stripping away the aspects of that style that render it a code to be initiated into, including peculiar "rules" almost designed to be broken, such as investing split infinitives with an air of suspicion (a friend wrote me recently asking whether it's okay to *begin* a sentence with a preposition!).

In Arab-speaking countries, the local dialects are viewed the same way as spoken Sinhalese, as "not real Arabic" in comparison to the standard taught in school and often incompletely mastered. However, in Egypt, the spoken variety is being mixed ever more with the standard in online writing. Most of us would look upon this approvingly, I suspect, as we would a similar process that has been happening in Sri Lanka. This leaves the question as to why we feel so different about codes mixing here in our own language.

Who says writing—and, more precisely, formal writing—is "realer" than the way we talk? Upon what did they base their argument? Upon the fact that, well, in the old days people wrote more formally? Well, given how little we do anything formally today, clearly the terms of the argument have changed. Or is their argument based, ultimately, on the fact that print is physically permanent while speech is evanescent? When technology emerges—i.e., word processing and its rapidity—that allows spoken style to be regularly imprinted permanently as well, then again, the terms of the argument must change.

OPINIONS WILL DIFFER on such matters, but not on a basic truth about language. Writing is a fifty-five-hundred-year-old process of freezing letters onto a page, applied to just a few of six thousand languages. Speaking is a process of producing sounds that likely dates back to the dawn of humanity and is inherent to the existence of every language on earth. If one of these processes has any claim to authenticity, writing is certainly not the one.

We are now ready to address the final aspect of language in our IDIOM acronym, which is about the fact that languages are not only ingrown but inbred.

CHAPTER FIVE

LANGUAGE IS MIXED

Of the five major Romance languages, Romanian is the odd one out. After some experience with French, Spanish, Italian, and/or Portuguese, take a crack at Romanian or even just try to read some, and it turns out to be (1) pretty in a Sophia Lorenish way (don't ask me why, but it's always been my impression, even though Loren is Italian), and (2) full of words that don't match with their equivalents in the other languages. You're used to words like *aimer*, *amar*, and *amare* for *love*, only to find that the Romanian word is *iubi*. You're waiting for a word like *temps* or *tiempo* for *time*, but instead it's some word seemingly out of nowhere, like *ceas*.

A Romanian I once knew had mixed feelings about this. She had learned enough French to notice that most of the words were familiar from her language, but that so very many were not. She wanted to know why, and I told her that it was because Romanian had developed farther to the east than French and crew, among people who also spoke Slavic languages. She couldn't help feeling that this made Romanian somehow impure. As she memorably put it (in an accent that sounded rather like Sophia Loren's—maybe that's part of my visceral personification of the language), "I don't want it to be that my language was a slut."

We will treat that word as gender-neutral, such that Wilt Chamberlain and Warren Beatty fall under its definition. It even began as a word about both sexes, as a reference to a messy person in general. Chaucer, in "The Canon Yeoman's Tale," refers to a man as "sluttish" ("Why is thy lord so sluttish, I thee preye?"). Plus, as late as the seventeenth century, when applied to a woman, the word could mean just "high-spirited"—from a modern perspective, one of the oddest entries in Samuel Pepys's diary is "Our little girl Susan is a most admirable slut, and pleases us mightily."

In that older meaning, we can accept that in the sense that Romanian was "a slut," all languages are. To the extent that the history of humankind has been so much a story of migration, languages have constantly come together. People worldwide have spoken more than one of them as a norm since time immemorial, such that the sense Americans have that speaking more than one language is worthy of remark is atypical. And because it is so utterly mundane that people are bilingual, languages mix. Language is, inherently, mixed.

EVERYBODY'S DOING IT: LANGUAGE MIXTURE AS A NORM

In Europe, for instance, the immigration of Indo-European language speakers from what is now either the Ukraine or Turkey extinguished the languages of the people who had occupied the continent for millennia before that. Basque, straddling France and Spain, is all that remains of what once was a more widespread family of languages, for example. After this, European history is riddled with migrations, amidst the spread of the Roman Empire, and then the invasion of the Huns and Avars from the east, the movements of Germanic and Slavic tribes to escape them (what the Germans call the grand *Völkerwanderung*), and the Roman Empire's breakdown in the wake of this. All of this meant new bilingualism and multilingualism, and thus more language mixing—today's European languages are all full of words from other ones, mostly now dead themselves. Moreover, that was just Europe. Endless movement was happening on the other continents as well.

Thus the language mixture created by transoceanic migrations and transplantations of massive numbers of people, of the kind possible and common only in the past several centuries, is merely part of an ongoing story. Languages worldwide have been cooking down together for a very, very long time.

The Romanian case seems remarkable only because it's the odd man out in its group, as an accident of geography. *Iubi* for *love* is cognate to words like Russian's *ljubit'* (just shave off the *l*), and the *ceas* word for *time* seems less odd when we know that the way to ask the time in Russian is *kotoryj čas?*, "which time?" The Slavic flavor of Romanian is perhaps most neatly encapsulated in the simple fact that the word for yes is *da*. (For the record, the Slavic languages that infected Romanian were actually not the East Slavic clan that includes Russian, but the South Slavic one that now contains Serbo-Croatian and Bulgarian.)

Yet the other Romance languages were "high-spirited" in their youth like Romanian was, just in different company. Take a Latin word like *antebellum*: *bellum* is the part that means "war," of course. And there is the expression *casus belli*, "case for war." So if the Latin word for *war* is *bellum*, then what's with French's *guerre*, Spanish's *guerra*, and so on?

That is actually from a word in the speech of the Franks, who spoke a language related to German and Dutch (and thus English) and were among the groups who moved southward and gradually nudged the Roman Empire into its downfall. Frankish for *war* was *werra*; over time a *g* crept into how the *w* was pronounced, and there's your *guerre*, *guerra*. (Elsewhere, *werra* became the word *war* that we are familiar with.) In the same way, if *dance* is *bailar* in Spanish and *ballare* in Italian, what's with *danser* in French—or even Italian's alternate *danzare*? French and Italian didn't get that from English, but from an early cousin of English—Frankish again, where the word was *dansōn*.

As you might guess, even the very name of France is based on the word *Frank*, meaning that what *la belle France* calls itself is a word from a language that was related to German.

The story is the same everywhere. We saw how it likely unfolded on Flores with the incursion of Tukang Besi words. And English, of course, is famously shot through with words unknown in Old English, from Norse, French, Dutch, Latin, and Greek especially. This is often presented as something special about English, but it isn't, really—language worldwide is mixed. It's an inevitable result of being one of six thousand languages on one small planet.

TO MIX, IT HELPS IF CLOTHES COME OFF

How this mixture looks different underwater is that it's about more than words. Often a language is described as a mixture of two or more just on the basis of vocabulary, but words are just clothes, not the body. Bukharan Jews,* for example, have their homeland in Uzbekistan; their language, although they also speak Russian, is Bukhori. It is often described as a "mixture of Persian, Russian, and Hebrew," but that only makes sense if a language is just words. Bukhori is, quite simply, a kind of Persian—the grammar is Persian's, in the same way as Afghanistan's Dari is a kind of Persian. More specifically, it is a variety of the third major Persian dialect, Tajik. Bukhori is a kind of Tajik Persian with, predictably, given who speaks it and where they live, a great many words from Hebrew and Russian (plus, equally predictably, Uzbek and some Arabic). It is a variety of

---

* For some reason, many barbers in New York are Bukharan. Before settling on the Haitian man who I go to now, I went to several Bukharan ones back in the day; they seemed to just keep popping up where I happened to be. One of them once shaved me nearly bald when I had not requested it. Others, however, did no such thing.

Judeo-Persian in the same way that Yiddish arose as a form of Judeo-German and Ladino is a form of Judeo-Spanish.

We are less likely to think of English as "a mixture of Viking, French, Dutch, Latin, and English" just because of its vocabulary. This is because while we speak English and are readily aware that it is a grammar as well as a lexicon, what stands out for us in other languages is the words alone—not to mention that there can be an idea that some languages "don't have grammar," like Twi. Yet the fact is that languages mix much more deeply than in just trading words like baseball cards. Languages fuse completely and create new ones that did not exist before, just as cells' mitochondria began as independent bacteria and made their home in other ones, producing today's cells that use mitochondria as energy generators (it's why mitochondria have their own DNA).

One of my favorite truly mixed languages is spoken in western China, where Mandarin Chinese has been used in mouths that also used Tibetan and even Mongolian, too.* Here's how to say *Let's look at it together*:

ŋa'mθ jita'tsɪ ji'ta'-kʰan-tœ.

You don't have to know Mandarin to see that this is a pretty weird kind of Chinese, from what we have already seen in this book. Chinese is *analytic*—barely any prefixes and suffixes. Yet there is clearly something prefixal or suffixal going on here in that last word. Plus, Chinese words tend to be short—one syllable, two syllables—which means that even that second word looks long.

What's happening here is, first, that the root words are from Mandarin, but they are bulked up with Tibetan roots alongside.

---

* Mongolian is part of one of three branches of a grand old family we have not met in this book, called Altaic. Another branch is the one that has Turkish on it, plus its line of close "Silk Road" relatives one hears about occasionally without quite knowing how they fit in. They include languages of the "Stan" countries: Uzbek, Kazakh, Kyrgyz. Azerbaijani and Tatar are also in this set.

On top of this, Mongolian is a language all about suffixes, and this language's grammar is on a Mongolian plan. Hence a suffix at the end, which has a particle-style meaning of conveying attitude—and because Mongolian keeps verbs at the end of sentences, so does this language.

It's called Wutun, and here's the sentence again, where Mandarin parts are in regular font, Tibetan parts are in **bold**, and Mongolian parts are <u>underlined</u>:

ŋa'mθ	ji**ta'**tsɪ	ji'**ta'**-kʰan-<u>tœ</u>.
we	all of us all-	look-ATTITUDE
"Let's look at it together."		

Now, that's a mixed language! It's neither fish nor fowl nor foal. You could call it a kind of Chinese because of some of the words, but my, there's so much else there that it'd be like calling rock music a kind of ragtime. Learning to speak it would require many of the tools we would use to learn Mongolian, including mastering lists of suffixes and word order that puts verbs last as in Japanese. Then, Tibetans could surely claim ownership of the language as well—it's full of Tibetan words as well as Mandarin ones, and Wutun speakers self-identify not as Mongols but as Tibetans. Wutun is a mutt.

As it happens, situations akin to Wutun, where two or more languages have a child together, are hardly rare worldwide. We don't hear much about them as a rule, because they are usually languages of low status that are only used fitfully on the printed page.

Some are created by overpowered groups in response to forced relocation and segregation—Euro-African hybrid creole languages like Jamaican patois, Gullah "Geechee Talk," and Cape Verdean Creole Portuguese are examples. Others started as trade lingos and made their way into the fabric of society as a handy way for people of different groups to communicate, but with native languages seen as more "real" in the sense described in Chapter Four. The kind of English that the Bloody Mary character in *South Pacific* speaks is a fictional refraction of an actual full-blown language of its own, one part English and one part the structural game plan of languages of Australian Aborigines and Melanesian islanders. It is used among indigenous people in Australia, New Guinea, and various islands eastward. Depending on where you are, it's called Kriol, Tok Pisin (*Pisin* is from the word *business*), Pijin, or, wouldn't you just know it, "Broken."*

---

* People familiar with lingua francas in this part of the world may find it unexpected that I group Australian Aboriginal Kriol with Tok Pisin, Solomon Islands Pijin, and (by implication) Vanuatu's Bislama. However, historical research over the past couple of decades has conclusively shown that all of these languages started with the Australian version, and structurally, the Australian version is similar enough to the others (once you get beyond the Australian vocabulary borrowings, which are just clothing, so to speak) that it is essentially a variation on the pattern more familiar from the extensive scholarship on Tok Pisin.

In other cases, hybrid generations of interethnic marriages create a Wutun-esque affair as a badge of in-group fellowship. There was, of all things, a cross between Russian and one of the Eskimo languages of the Yupik sort from Chapter One, when Russian traders had children with local women.

Such mixed languages are typically seen as lesser versions of other ones—Jamaican as "bad English," for example, a judgment leveled at it as ruthlessly as the equivalent one about Black English is in America. Urban Nigerians, aside from indigenous languages, speak a creole English descended from Jamaican and Gullah, via a transportation of slaves *back* to Sierra Leone in Africa after the Revolutionary War. That is, a person from Kingston and a person from Lagos could converse in a language that to most of us would be barely comprehensible beyond the occasional recognizable word.* A speaker of this *language* will typically dismiss it as "broken English," when its grammatical description in fact runs hundreds of pages, and learning to speak this "broken" language would be a matter of lessons, practice, endless mistakes, and never truly sounding native, just as with any other language.

Urban Ghanaians speak a variation of the same thing—but this has only been widely known and studied in recent years, as Ghanaians, too, think of it as "not a real language." I will never forget a conversation with a Ghanaian Twi speaker who also spoke this "broken" English, where I was pointing out some of

---

* My first time hearing a creole language spoken was one of the twenty-five or so most marvelous, memorable, and downright disorienting experiences of my life. It was Jamaican patois, and all I could tell was that I could get a lot of the words as English but somehow couldn't follow what the two people were saying no matter how hard I listened. I assume that having a stroke must feel rather like this. Pointedly, when I politely asked the people what they were speaking, the response was ambivalent. They thought of themselves as speaking a kind of English, which they were, depending on where you draw the line—although it was a lot further from Standard English than Black English is. But this was an English with a very touchy reputation in Jamaica, such that it isn't everyone who will readily and openly say "We're speaking Patois!" as someone might say "We're speaking Thai!" It was very Chapter Four.

its grammatical constructions and she was sweetly bemused that I would dwell on what she thought of as about as worthy of attention as an American would think of Pig Latin being.

Such mixed languages sometimes do acquire enough legitimacy to be written and used in the public sphere. Tok Pisin in Papua New Guinea—the eastern half of the island, where Indonesian is unknown—is the language of governance and there is a newspaper in it. However, even in such cases, the language is almost never glimpsed on paper or even heard beyond where it is spoken, as representatives from the area use a Major Language when in the wider world.

CASE STUDY: THE REAL LANGUAGE SITUATION IN SRI LANKA

Yet from a linguist's underwater perspective, language mutts are a regular part of the linguistic landscape, often obscured by language maps and official language designations that imply that there are only "pure" languages, usually written ones. A handy microcosm of this is, in fact, Sri Lanka. So far I have left you to suppose that Sri Lanka is home to exactly two languages, both of them discrete "pure" entities, with a writing tradition stretching far back in time: Sinhalese and Tamil. Of course, I did fill in some of the reality in showing that Sinhalese is really two languages, the antique written version and the modern spoken one. The Tamil situation, for the record, is not unlike it. But even this only scratches the surface of a situation that is all about languages mixing together.

FOR ONE, TAKE SINHALESE ITSELF. Like its Indo-Aryan sister languages, such as Hindi, Sinhalese seems distinctly unlike what we think of as an Indo-European language. The verb coming at the end always, for example, as in the *The man sees the* *elephant* sentence from Chapter Four, is nothing like what we are used to in French or even Russian.

Miniha-ṭə	aliyawə	peenəwa.
man-to	elephant	sees

There is also the sound of it. The dot under the *t* in this sentence indicates that the *t* is pronounced with the tongue pulled slightly back. Indo-Aryan languages have a number of consonants like that, and they are part of what creates their sonic flavor. But Western European languages don't harbor collections of these sounds, called retroflex (which sounds, I know, like one of those ThighMaster gadgets, but isn't).

In this and other ways, Sinhalese and its relatives have a different overall plan than most Indo-European languages. The reason is because millennia ago, earlier Indo-Aryan languages were learned by speakers of the other language family of the subcontinent, Dravidian. Dravidian is a completely different family from Indo-European, as distinct from it as Semitic or Austronesian, and it originally covered the area.

But Indo-European speakers moved in, gradually pressing southward, with the result of today's situation, where Dravidian holds on in the south, with just a few isolated patches surviving up north as an indication of its original spread. This all meant extensive and long-term interaction between Indo-European and Dravidian peoples, and still does. It would have been quite odd if the Indo-European languages of the area had come out of all of this without a heavy infusion of Dravidianality. Nothing odd happened, and as such, just as Dravidian languages keep the verb at the end and have retroflex consonants, so do languages like Sinhalese. Its cohabitation of a small island with Dravidian Tamil has only furthered this stewing since. Sinhalese, therefore, is a mixed language itself.

And not only with Dravidian. In addition, the Sinhalese speakers met an aboriginal group when they got to the island, the Veddas, some of whom survive today. The Veddas have long spoken a variety of Sinhalese; their original language is extinct and was never written for posterity. However, Sinhalese is full of words that match with no cognates in its Indo-Aryan relatives up north, like Hindi, and are the heritage of Veddas picking up Sinhalese in antiquity and peppering it with their own words, as Yiddish speakers gave English words like *schlemiel*. Body-part words are common among these words for some reason. Sinhalese's *olluva*, "head," *kakula*, "leg," and *bella*, "neck," would not feel like variants on their own words to a Hindi or Bengali speaker in the way that French's *main* makes immediate sense to a Spaniard or Italian with their *mano*. Even the name of Sri Lanka's capital, Colombo, traces back to a Vedda word for *harbor*. Adult Veddas were no more likely to learn perfect Sinhalese than we would be, and thus Sinhalese has vocabulary mix-ins from Vedda on top of its grammatical seasoning from Dravidian.

BUT WAIT, THERE'S MORE! Sri Lanka, due to its geographical location, has been the scene of trade and colonization by many powers. First in line were the Portuguese, whose immense geopolitical sway in the sixteenth and seventeenth centuries always seems so counterintuitive given the modest, almost obscure status of little Portugal in modern times. The Portuguese got to the island in 1517, having scoped it out from India, where they were already established. Over the next hundred years, they took commercial control of much of the island, while, as was the tendency in the era, also preaching their religion—Catholicism, and in Portuguese.

Soon there was a generation of descendants of Portuguese traders and local women. Between them and the influence of the Portuguese religious instruction, Portuguese was now spoken in Sri Lanka alongside Sinhalese and Tamil. It still is, by a small number of people.

However, it is not the Portuguese of Lisbon. First of all, it is simplified Portuguese—few were in a position, or of an inclination, to learn the entire grammar itself. All Sri Lankans, even the "half-castes," had their own Sinhalese or Tamil. Then, it is also Portuguese as filtered through Sinhalese grammar. Or Tamil grammar; there's barely a meaningful difference in terms of the Sri Lankan Portuguese result, because Sinhalese and Tamil have been brewing together for so long that their grammars are similar—a microcosm of the Indo-Aryan/Dravidian "marriage" in a broader sense.

So: Sinhalese, remember, has a way of making it explicit when something is happening to someone rather than them doing it, even though in both cases, the someone is the subject of the sentence and English just leaves it there. Seeing is *to* a man:

Miniha-țə	aliyawə	peenəwa
man-to	elephant	sees

Sri Lankan Portuguese has that same tic, except with Portuguese words, *Do you want?* comes out as "You have desire?":

Bos ten dizey?

That seems familiar enough, but I cheated a bit—it's slightly incomplete. Actually, you add *to* to the *bos* pronoun *you*. *To* is *pa* (from Portuguese's *para* for *for*). Thus because desire happens *to* you:

Bos-**pa** ten dizey? "Do you want?"

It's Sinhalese in Portuguese clothing. To say *Now he also asks the bride*, you put the verb at the end, just as a good Indo-Aryan or Dravidian language likes it:

Awara	osir	tan	noiyva-nt	a	**lo-punta**.
now	he	also	bride-on	to	**ask**

"Now he also asks the bride."

And in *noiyva-nt*, "bride-on," we see that this is a Portuguese word that has case suffixes as if it were trying to stay like its Latin parent. It's because Sinhalese has such suffixes. The *-nt* means *on*, because as it happens, in Sri Lankan Portuguese you "ask on" someone instead of just asking them. Prepositions are capricious even within one language—note that some English speakers say *wait on* someone instead of *wait for*. But if *ask on* were how to say it in the Portuguese of Europe or Brazil, the *on* would be a preposition as in English, sitting before what was asked on and separate from it—ask *on* the bride. The *-nt* suffix for *on* is based on a Portuguese word, to be sure—*junto* for *joined*—but it's used for a Sinhalese purpose and in a Sinhalese way. Naturally, people whose way of saying *to the man* is "man-to," *miniha-ṭə*, will build "bride-on" as *noiyva-nt*.

This is Sinhalese in Portuguese, then—but that's only a partial characterization of what this language is. In this "bride" sentence, for example, the words are almost all from Portuguese, but Portuguese as heard by non-native speakers in a context where language is mostly an oral business, with reading and writing in the language a marginal activity. Thus *osir* is from the Portuguese *o senhor*, "the gentleman," used as a term of respect like Spanish's *usted*. *Tan* is how we might transcribe *também*, "also," if hearing it on the fly uttered rapidly in a language we knew nothing of. *Punta* is from *preguntar*—again, a natural version of that word without the artificial tether of seeing it written out when we say it.

Sri Lankan Portuguese is a cross between Portuguese and Sinhalese (and Tamil), then, but also a simplification of them all. Despite the case suffixes on nouns, there is nothing like that plethora of verb forms we saw for colloquial Sinhalese ("not the real language"!!!), and Sri Lanka Portuguese does not have crazy European-style gender or the sticky conjugational endings (complete with three classes and ample irregular verbs) that Portuguese has.

Yet as we have seen, a language doesn't have to have endings or even tones to be as intricate—"real"—as English or any other, and Sri Lanka Portuguese has, in any case, a certain number of endings regardless. This kind of language, a product of mixture but also simplification, is what many linguists term a creole language. This means that Sri Lanka is home not only to Sinhalese and Tamil, but to a language born amidst adults' eternal handicap in learning new languages completely but maintaining its essence as a real language. That is, as in putting subjects in separate drawers according to whether they do something or experience it.

Sri Lanka is home to two languages like that, actually. The Dutch, long established eastward in what is today Indonesia, naturally eyed Sri Lanka and eased aside the Portuguese there, starting in the seventeenth century. The Portuguese had brought slaves to Sri Lanka from their entrepôts in east Africa; these slaves also helped create Sri Lanka Portuguese. The Dutch brought slaves in as well, but from Java. These were Malay speakers, as were the Javanese soldiers the Dutch also brought over.

They stayed on, and had children with local women just as the Portuguese traders had. Soon there was a new brand of Malay reflecting the heritage of the new generation: Malay spoken in Sinhalese, basically. Some few still speak it. Once again, there is that fondness for marking the *to*-nesses of life. *Lorang* is *you*; *lorang-nang* is *to you*. This same *nang* peeks out from how you say *They heard a familiar voice*:

Derang-**nang**	byaasa	svaara	hatthu	su-dinggar.
they-to	habit	voice	a	heard

"They heard a familiar voice."

Hearing is an experience; in Sri Lanka Malay it happens *to them* or, more properly, *them to—derang-nang*.* And of course the verb *heard* comes at the end—Sinhalese in, this time, Malay.

---

* Traditionally it has been assumed that only Tamil and not Sinhalese was the basis for Sri Lanka Malay's grammatical patterns. The evidence for this, however, would appear to have been more an assertion passed down than a demonstrated conclusion. I find the source by Umberto Ansaldo I have listed in the bibiography convincing on this score.

Yet just as in Sri Lanka Portuguese Creole, there is not the full baroque plethora of endings in Sinhalese despite its reproduction of the *to* fetish. Plus, the men from Java already spoke the simplified kind of Malay that made the linguistic aspect of my trip to Papua so pleasant. Simplify two languages, wind them up, and watch them go—as a language like any other, albeit taking it lighter.

FINALLY, THE WAY THE ABORIGINAL VEDDA speak Sinhalese is another thing entirely. Still Sinhalese, basically, but a Sinhalese in distinctly unique garb to say the least, to the point that it is typically referred to as a separate "Vedda language."

It's the oddest thing: nouns tend to come out with suffixes that they don't have in regular Sinhalese. And not just short little suffixes, like *-s* and *-pa* and *-nt*, that don't call too much attention to themselves, but long, aggressive suffixes that seem to "want" to be heard. In Vedda Sinhalese, nouns wear really loud socks, basically.

	Sinhalese	**Vedda Sinhalese**
nose	naase	naaspojja
ear	kana	kanrukula
leg	kakula	kakuldanḍa
water	diya	diyaraacca
worm	paṇiyā	pannilääto
head	iha	ijjejja

What are these *-rukula* / *-raacca* / *-pojja* thingies? What in the world are these big, fat suffixes doing dangling off the ends of the nouns like that? They're not in Sinhalese or in any Indo-Aryan language.

Well, not technically. But as it turns out, the suffixes are based on Sinhalese words for things like nuts and sticks and heaps. And for littleness. You apply the suffix depending on which of those qualities the noun has. Is anything we've seen in previous chapters coming to mind?

	Sinhalese	Vedda	Sinhalese source
nose	naase	naaspojja	poḍḍa "a little"
ear	kana	kanrukula	rukula "support, stay"
leg	kakula	kakuldanḍa	danḍa "stick"
water	diya	diyaraacca	raasiya "heap"
worm	paṇiyā	pannilääto	eeääto "those people"
head	iha	ijjejja	geḍiya "nut"

Vedda Sinhalese is as if in English we heard someone fluently talking about how once someone poured a water-heap on their head-nut and they accidentally snorted it up their nosy, or how once after gardening, they found a worm-person crawling on their leg-stick.

As bizarre as that would sound to us, it makes sense if we think of the classifiers in Chinese. The question, after all, is why the Vedda are so mad to do this when other speakers of Indo-Aryan languaes aren't. Hindi, Punjabi, Sinhalese, and the rest may be their own special brand of Indo-European in many ways, but they do not go as far as having flatties of bed and bubbles of buttons. Bengali and Assamese do, to an extent, but only from rubbing up against unrelated languages next door that have them. Generally, when Indo-Aryan languages subdivide nouns into classes, it's in good old-fashioned Indo-European style, with little masculine-feminine endings (and sometimes neuter).

This means that these argyle suffixes must have something to do with the now-lost language that the Veddas originally spoke. We will never know its grammatical structure in detail, but one thing we can see is that it must have been a language with classifiers—which is not a surprise as so many languages of Southeast Asia just nearby still are. The Vedda who switched from their original language to Sinhalese rendered it with equivalents to the classifiers they were used to. As an isolated group, the Vedda have always been speaking more to one another than to Sinhalese or Tamil speakers, and thus this Vedda-infused kind of Sinhalese could settle in without being dismissed as incorrect or funny-sounding by outsiders.*

That historical scenario explains other things about Vedda Sinhalese,† such as that it has more than a few Sinhalese words that haven't been used since the 1100s and are now otherwise only found in ancient Sinhalese texts of that era. The everyday use among the Vedda of *devla* for *sky* and *diyamacca* for *fish* is as if the same people talking about their leg-sticks were dropping in Old English words here and there on top of that, referring to the sky as the *lyft*, for example. Much of what determines which words go out of fashion and which hold on is chance. After the Veddas started using Sinhalese in their own way, chance operated differently on their rendition's vocabulary than on the more general one. In a situation like that, after fifteen hundred years, you're in for some *lyft*, not to mention some water-heaps up your nosy.

---

* Funny, though—they only hung the classifiers on Sinhalese words, rather than the ones remaining from their original Vedda language. It's as if they were trying to give themselves a leg up in remembering what these new Sinhalese words meant.

† Yes, Sinhalese and Vedda specialists, I'm going to call it that. I know that some have termed it a creole because it's mixed, but that overextends the definition of *creole* to an extent that renders it useless. Countless languages mix grammar, just as Sinhalese itself and its sister languages like Hindi were born of a mixture of Indo-Aryan and Dravidian; probably *most* languages mix grammar. The Veddas' Sinhalese is mixed with (some) constructions from the original Vedda language, but does not simplify Sinhalese to any remarkable extent in the way that Sri Lanka Portuguese simplifies Portuguese. "Vedda language" is, basically, a kind of Sinhalese with Vedda decorations. It is mixed, but not creole, to the extent that creoles are also born in radical simplification. Designations of the Veddas' Sinhalese as "creole" were put forth decades ago when the study of language contact and the taxonomization of its various results were less advanced. I hereby propose a revision.

JUST ADD WATER AND STIR:
BORN-AGAIN MIXED LANGUAGES

Language mixture is not only ordinary, but harmless. A blend of two or more languages is not compromised, in the way that a cross between a horse and a donkey is a sterile mule. It could seem that a combination of a portion of one language and a portion of another is fundamentally incomplete. One sometimes senses that impression even in speakers of saliently mixed languages, who are not unknown to say, "Oh, it's just some English with some Spanish and some other things mixed in." "Just"—not "real." Too, shall we say, friendly. Not respectable.

Not so. Language is like the life force in a way. If a language exists—that is, if mentally uncompromised and mature human beings speak it casually and effortlessly to express their humanity—then it is always a coherent and complex system. One will hear that all languages are *equally* complex, but that is, frankly, absurd. There is no reason that they would be, and no one with a modicum of experience with a range of the world's languages could seriously make such a claim. Ket is more grammatically complex than Indonesian, period. All languages are, however, complex to a degree. Mixture cannot touch this, and a beautiful example of this is the creole language Saramaccan—because it's an example of how language lives on even amidst not only mixture but destruction.

Created by adult slaves in the late seventeenth century, it was born from vast simplification—a Persian Conversion of epic scale. There are no conjugational endings and no case-marking suffixes, no classifiers, and no fencing off subjects in sentences with transitive verbs from subjects in sentences with intransitive ones. It has tones because it was created by Africans who spoke tonal languages, but almost never the kind that by themselves make the difference between words. Saramaccan has nothing like Akha's *ma* meaning "mother," "full," "not," "dream," or "group" depending on what pitch and timbre you

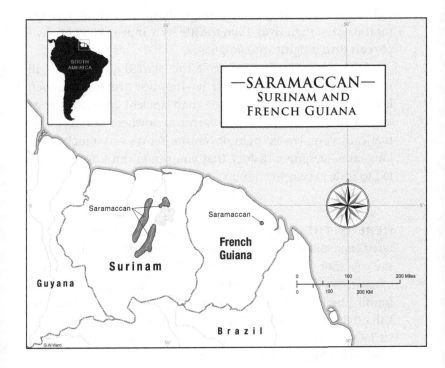

pronounce it with. For the most part, high tone just goes where the word's accent is. *Walk* is *wáka*; that's pronounced WAH-kah, and the WAH is also pronounced on a higher tone than the kah. But that's not so unlike how an English speaker would say *wáka*. You could speak Saramaccan without the tones and sound foreign but understandable; try speaking Chinese without tones and you risk calling people's mothers horses.

This is because Saramaccan, like Sri Lanka Portuguese and Malay, is a creole. It started as a way for adults to communicate despite how hard it is to learn new languages after the teen years. A creole often begins this way, as a deliberately simple kind of code, with a limited vocabulary and as little "grammar" as possible. In terms of the essence of language as we have seen it in this book, that means that a creole can start as something that *isn't* a language at all. It's a pidgin. But if the pidgin is the only handy way people are going to have for communication for the rest of their lives, then the life force indeed kicks in. People can turn pidgins into languages.

A few centuries later, a creole that started as a pidgin will still have hallmarks of that birth—they are structurally much less frustrating to a newcomer than ancient languages (e.g., almost all of the others). Saramaccan is nowhere near as grammatically complex as Archi or Navajo. Yet it's very much a real language—despite a history that you would think would have led to little except word soup.

HERE IS THE SCENE: King Charles I has just been decapitated, and during the Interregnum Period of English history, the governor of the Barbados colony, Lord Willoughby, sees that elbow room is running short on that little island and sets sail to found a new colony on the coast of Surinam in 1651. The English establish plantations there and staff them with slaves from various points on the west African coast, as well as colonies they have already set up, like Barbados.

Soon, the slaves are speaking a creole, especially since the slaves taken from Barbados already spoke one. The words are English. The grammar, because quite a few of the slaves being brought from Africa come from Togo and Benin, is partly English and partly the Fongbe we met in Chapter Three—but a simplified version of both, used as the yeast for the rising of a new language. This only lasts, however, for a little more than fifteen years.

In America, we are often aware that the Dutch were the original occupants of New York (as New Netherland) and that in 1667, amidst a peace treaty, they yielded it to the English. We are less aware that this was part of a wider arrangement involving a swap whereby the English gave up Surinam down in South America to the Dutch. The arrangement was that the English had to leave their slaves along with the plantations. From now on, the slaves on Surinam's plantations are working under Dutch masters. But their in-group creole with English words is already formed; there's no reason to scrap it and put together a new one with Dutch words. The slaves learn some Dutch, and the Dutch go pretty far in learning the creole. Naturally some Dutch words trickle into the English creole, but only that.

Meanwhile, two years before the big trade-off, in 1665, a third European contingent came to this small colony: Portuguese plantation owners. Specifically, they were Jewish ones on the run from the Inquisition in their home country. Having found Brazil suddenly uncongenial after the Portuguese took it over from the Dutch, they settled on the eastern half of Surinam's coast. They bought many slaves from the English and likely already had some of their own. Soon they also brought new slaves in from Africa.

Plantation work in Surinam, especially on sugar plantations, which were so brutal as to be virtual death sentences, had a way of encouraging slaves to escape. *Con sangre se hace azúcar*, "Sugar is made with blood," as it was said in Spanish colonies. In Surinam, it was useful to this end that the interior is a rain forest. Slaves quickly started fleeing both Dutch and Portuguese plantations and making new lives in the forest. We would hope that they would have somehow made their way back to Africa, but in reality, this was the rest of their lives. We can only consider it lucky that quite a few of the escapees had not even had to spend much time on the plantations.

And now, a question: in a rain forest settlement of African slaves who escaped from, say, the Portuguese plantations, what would the people speak? Or—the descendants of those escapees still live right there in Surinam, numbering about twenty-four thousand, in villages mostly along the Saramacca River. What do they speak? English? Portuguese? Dutch?

None of them. No one in Surinam spoke English after 1667. As for Dutch, few of the slaves from the Portuguese plantations had ever heard it either. As for speaking Portuguese itself, how much quality time had most escaped slaves even spent with Portuguese people, given the hideous work requirements of plantation labor? Portuguese *words*? Sure. But the language itself? For all but the slaves working in the house or thereabouts, probably not.

Do their descendants now speak an African language, then? In the visual and cultural sense, you might expect that they would. In broad outlines, an "African" culture has been preserved in the Surinamese rain forest over the past three centuries in terms of dress, dance, ceremonial practices, and art forms. Black Surinamese on the coast today even refer to the blacks who live in the interior as "Africans" sometimes. But they do not speak an African language, except for three that are used in frozen form for ceremonial purposes.

And the fact that there are three of those is part of why no one of them is the everyday language. The original slaves spoke several African languages, and there was no reason for any single one of them to be adopted as the language of preference. How would they have chosen one? On what grounds would those whose language was not chosen have simply knuckled under? Why would a Fongbe speaker assent to having to learn Twi? Or even if Fongbe happened to have gotten in on the ground early on, such that Saramaccan grammar is based on it, why would Twis who came later bow down to Fongbe?

For better or for worse, the most plausible, culture-neutral lingua franca for these Africans would have to be a European one. But which one? Certainly, a rendition of European created by Africans themselves on the model of an African language would make a certain sense. Slaves from the Portuguese plantations had been exposed to the English-Fongbe creole of the original slaves now working with them, sprayed with a heavy coat of Dutch words after the change of ownership under the 1667 treaty, which had then been subjected to an outright deluge of Portuguese words when adopted by slaves on those plantations. And this hybrid, this creole language, was exactly what the slaves learned and spoke with one another on Portuguese plantations. Their descendants in the rain forest still do.*

UNLIKE MOST CREOLES, which take most of their words from one language, usually West European, Saramaccan is so mixed that it doesn't lend itself to any kind of conception as a poor man's version of something else. It's not a kind of English, it's not a kind of Portuguese, and despite its many African words as well as African-style grammar, no African would recognize it as a version of their language, not even a Fongbe speaker. Saramaccan is just Saramaccan. Here's a sentence, from a folktale:

Nɔɔ hɛ̃́ wɛ   wã́ dáka,   dí mujɛ́ɛ-míi   tá-fõ   pindá.
So   then   one day   the woman-child   was-beating peanut
"So then one day the girl was crushing peanuts."

In this one sentence, wã́ and dí are from English, as is nɔɔ, which started out as *no more*, and hɛ̃́, which started as *then*. *Mujɛ́ɛ-míi* is from Portuguese's *mulher* and *menino*. *Dáka* is from Dutch's *dag*. *Wɛ* and *fõ* are Fongbe words, and *pindá* is from the Kikongo language of Angola, where a great many other Surinam

---

* Meanwhile, black people on the coast, descendants of the slaves who stayed on Dutch plantations, still speak that basic English-Fongbe creole, now called Sranan, which lacks the Portuguese element of Saramaccan and has words mostly from English, with a heavy later-on incorporation from Dutch. Sranan is now the vernacular lingua franca of Surinam, spoken by all, including people of Indian, Chinese, and Javanese descent; one sometimes hears of it as "taki-taki." There are also rain forest communities established by escapees from the Dutch plantations as opposed to the Portuguese ones. They speak a variation of Sranan called Ndjuka or, more properly, four dialects thereof. You would not know that any of these languages existed from the almanac status of Dutch as "the" language of Surinam. My preferred book of data on Countries of the World at least lists "Pidgin English" for Sranan and, I suppose, Ndjuka (although making them sound like they aren't actual languages: the grammatical description of Ndjuka by my friends George and Mary Huttar is a doorstop) and "Saramacca" (close, at least!).

slaves came from (in the United States a dialect name for peanuts is *pinders*, because of this Kikongo word). Of course Saramaccan speakers have no access to this now archival information:
this is, for them, their vocabulary, period.

The way Saramaccan works grammatically is basically Fongbe
lite. If I had been stopped by an airport security worker at the airport in Surinam's capital, Paramaribo, and asked him whether I
could finish my water, I would have said:

Mi   sá   bebé   ế   kabá   akí   ɔ́?
I   can   drink   it   finish here   QU
"Can I drink it here?"

I would have run *drink* and *finish* together without a word
like *and*, as Fongbe would in a sentence like *I take crab put table on*.
I would also have used a particle, ɔ́, for asking a question, because
it's not only Russian and Esperanto that do that, but Fongbe, too.

But *isn't* this, from what we have seen, word soup? One is
pardoned for having perhaps a quiet impression that there is an
air of baby talk about it on first glance, with the words mostly
ending in vowels, *me* for *I*, the verbs strung together, and perhaps more *b*'s than we're used to in that drinking sentence.

But it isn't word soup in the least.

CREOLE AS IDIOM

The miracle is that the product of that roiling history, where five
languages were thrown together to create a new language from
the ground up just a few hundred years ago, quickly became a
language like any other, which has to be "learnt." Although it's
so very mixed as well, Saramaccan has all four of the other fundamental features of language we have seen in this book.

It's *ingrown* in places, for example. The way I learned about
one aspect of that was from a strange way it uses a word for

throw. The word is *túwɛ*, which may not look much like *throw*, but it's what happened over time to a word that started out as *trowe*, "TRO-way," which you perhaps can glean *throw away* from: you pronounce *túwɛ* as "TOO-weh."

Túwɛ 101 is normal—*I threw the book* is *Mi túwɛ dí búku*. Then you can also use it in the kind of sentence where verbs are strung together like train cars. Another word for *throw* is *vínde*, and to say *I threw the book* you can also say:

Mi vínde dí búku túwɛ.

So you have two *throws*. A little odd, actually. But alone it hardly suggests anything "ingrown"—it just looks a little repetitious. Yet grappling with how anything in the world works requires ignoring what seems like static. Maybe using two *throws* like this is an "idiom," who knows? Like *Have a look-see*, maybe? I was interested in other things.

But grappling with the world also requires facing when something is less a matter of static than disorder, suggesting a major failure of understanding. *Túwɛ* actually pops up in sentences all the time in ways that don't seem to make any sense, and much too often for it to be a matter of random, disconnected idiom. There's something going on with *túwɛ* beyond mere throwing.

For example, to say *I cut the tree down*, you say "I felled the tree throw":

Mi fáa dí páu túwɛ.

But why "throw"? Surely Saramaka people do not have a cultural tradition involving first cutting a tree down and then picking it up and hurling it.

Well, just maybe there is some sense that to cut something down is a kind of throwing, which it is, kind of . . . but what about how they can say *I shot the pig*? It's "I shoot the pig throw."

Mi súti dí píngo túwɛ.

Again, what's thrown? Technically, the bullet, maybe—but just why is it that the Saramaka seem to have such an abstract, almost poetic sense of what throwing is? Is that really what's going on? The sentence that made me sure that it wasn't was this one, where someone describes birds having flown into his house and his chasing them out. It goes:

Mi	jáka	dí	fóu	túwɛ	a	dɔ́ɔ.
I	chase	the	bird	throw	at	outside

"I chased the birds out of the house."

Once again, this "throwing" business where it doesn't fit. You don't grab birds out of the air and hurl them. You just don't.*

I actually asked a Saramaccan speaker why he used *túwɛ* in this way. He had given this sentence:

Mi	tɔ́tɔ	dí	dágu	túwɛ	a	dí	wáta.
I	push	the	dog	throw	at	the	water

"I pushed the dog into the water."

(Note that the word for *push*, an African one, *tɔ́tɔ*, is also the name of a famous dog; that's just an accident.)

I wanted to get a sense of how something like this involved throwing. Once again, you could see the pushing as constituting a kind of throwing, but it seems strained. The notion of a people who would say "Any movement is, to us, a form of hurling" is possibly profound but also faintly insane.

---

* By the way, here is where I might note that Saramaccan has two kinds of *e* and two kinds of *o*. We saw the ɔ in Chapter Four from the International Phonetic Alphabet, meaning *aw* as opposed to *o* meaning *oh*. In the same way, ɛ is the International Phonetic Alphabet's *eh* as opposed to *e* meaning *ay*. Many Saramaccan sources indicate *eh* and *aw* as *ë* and *ö*. That, to me, is like the ĩ and ũ business we saw for Kikuyu in Chapter One to indicate *ay* and *oh*—nah.

I asked, "So is this about tossing the dog off the ship into the water or bending over and giving him a push?" (upon which I physically demonstrated the action). The speaker said it was definitely about pushing. So I cheated and actually asked him, "What does *túwɛ* mean in that sentence? And what does it *mean* when you use it to talk about chopping down trees?" And from the bemused look on his face and his saying, "I don't know, you just have to say it," I instantly knew what was up. It's *grammar!*

That is, the kind of thing speakers of a language do subconsciously without being able to explain it—systematic rule-bound practices of the kind that foreigners strain to learn. And that meant that *túwɛ* must, in these sentences, not "mean" anything. Rather, it must be encoding some abstract aspect of what is going on in the sentences, like tense, or graduality (like incrementally achieving a stench in Navajo)—but obviously not them.

And looking at all of the sentences with this abstract version of *túwɛ*, I could see what the function was. *Túwɛ* is used to indicate that something traveling through the air reaches an end point. We can think of it as meaning "thrown," or more precisely as "having reached the end state of having been thrown." If there were one word we could use to translate this usage of *túwɛ*, it might be *lands*. When a tree falls, it lands—the answer to "If a tree falls and no one is there to see it, does it land?" is yes. If you shoot a pig, the bullet has come to a stop in said pig. If you chase birds out of your house, eventually they end up—land—outside of it.

Even "I throw the book throw," *Mi vínde dí búku túwɛ*, makes sense now. It does not mean "I throw the book throw"—it means that I threw the book and it landed somewhere. *Mi vínde dí búku* alone just indicates that you hurled the book, and it could have disintegrated in the air for all we know—or you might put it that way if you threw the book in outer space where there was no gravity, so that the book couldn't land anywhere.

So, in the sentence with the dog, *Mi tɔ́tɔ dí dágu túwɛ a dí wáta*, *túwε* indicates that the dog landed. To say just *Mi tɔ́tɔ dí dágu a dí wáta* with no *túwε* refers, strictly speaking, to being in the water with the dog and giving him a push, I suppose to encourage him to swim, or because it's not your dog and you don't like him, or for whatever reason you'd do such a thing. It's *túwε* that makes the sentence about the dog flying through the air and hitting the water (and hopefully not encountering some wader who then pushes him away!).

This isn't as bizarre as it might seem. English can indicate the same thing with *into* as opposed to *in*. *I pushed the dog in the water* could mean either that you pushed the dog off a pier or that you were in the water and shoved the dog. *I pushed the dog into the water* can only mean the less charitable push off the pier; you couldn't say it if you and the dog were already in the water. Saramaccan is just stricter about marking that nuance, and in more cases of movement—rather as if in English we had to say *I shot into the pig dead* instead of just *I shot the pig* dead. Obviously Saramaka of an alternate universe could get along fine without saying things like *I shot into the pig*—but in this universe, the language happens to do so anyway.

In this way, then, Saramaccan is ingrown. The *túwε* business is, in fact, an inherited Fongbe-ism; in that language the verb for *throw* is used in a similar way. Saramaccan is a mixture, and it was also born in radical simplification, as it had to be. Yet because its parent languages had ingrownness, some of it rubbed off into Saramaccan as well, despite the general push toward streamlining. In Saramaccan, if you just say *I pushed the dog in the water*, you're technically being a little vague.

SARAMACCAN IS *DISSHEVELED*, TOO. Not extremely. Irregularities emerge from an accumulation of erosions and train wrecks over time. Saramaccan began as a pidgin, which is (1) deliberately easy and (2) doesn't really consist of much material at all. In something that is barely a system, there's little room for anything one could call irregular.* Real language though it became after that stage, Saramaccan has only had so much time to gunk up beyond it. But three centuries is far from nothing, and to speak Saramaccan is to find, for example, that the *be* verb is tricky.

If I say that I *am* myself, then I say *Mi da John*. But if I say that the dog *is* mine, then suddenly, no *be* is necessary.

Dí	dágu	u	mí.
The	dog	for	me

But then if I say *The dog is mine!* in an insistent way—perhaps in stopping those people from pushing him off things—I put it as "*Mine* is the dog," and suddenly I have to use a *be*. Yet, not the *da* from *Mi da John*, "I am John," but a shortened form, *a*, that you never use in any other context:

U	mí	**a**	dí	dágu!
For	me	is	the	dog

Go figure. It happened bit by bit, for reasons one can trace if one feels like it. But one usually does not, and in life as we know it, it's just irregular.

Saramaccan also has its *intricacies*—complexities of a kind

---

* There are those who consider it a gravely portentous error to say that plantation creoles began as pidgins. All agree that plantation creoles were born from abbreviation of a language; the question is how much. There is a hazy consensus at this point that creoles harbor what few would dispute when phrased as "the effects of second-language acquisition by adults." Because that alone also describes what created English, Persian, and Indonesian, I am here calling the more extreme extent to which it occurred to create a language like Saramaccan *pidginization*—i.e., like someone saying *Me Tarzan* instead of *I am Tarzan*. Many take this as implying that creoles even *now* are as primitive as the language of Tarzan, or that there was something wrong with people whose first rendition of a new language was like this. I doubt that readers of this book will glean that from what I have presented; if any have, please do not. Debate (especially if *standoff* is encompassed within the term *debate*) continues among specialists over the arcana of this issue, which I will spare you.

that don't seem apparent when a language doesn't work like Latin. Let's go back to this poor little dog just one more time. I guess I think he's little because the sentences have *tɔtɔ* in them. I'd therefore feel the same way if the word were *ásta* (the Thin Man dog, to return to that series) or *fála* (the Roosevelts' dog). Plus you don't imagine a Saint Bernard putting up with this kind of treatment for long. Anyway, *túwɛ* isn't the only verb that you can use both literally and with an abstract meaning. In this sentence, *púu*, "to pull," means not *pull*, but just *out of*:

A	tɔtɔ	dí	dágu	púu	a	dí	wági.
He	push	the	dog	"pull"	at	the	car

"He pushed the dog out of the car."

Obviously you can't be pulling a dog you are pushing (or if you are, then goodness, we're giving this animal a hard time!). Over time, *púu* came to mean just an abstract part of what pulling is, movement away from something else, even if it is being pushed instead of pulled.

But when it comes to how you use little *púu*, Saramaccan is starting to distinguish verbs that take objects from verbs that don't. If you thought you had *púu* figured out and wanted to say that you walked out of the house, then certainly you'd say:

Mi	wáka	púu	a	dí	wósu.
I	walk	out	at	the	house

"I walked out of the house."

Or not. That'd be "cute" Saramaccan, like the time I heard a Bulgarian say, *After all, you two are the ones who are the early-waking-up-persons!* to refer to their being early risers. It was processible— you *could* say that in English. But you just don't. In uncute Saramaccan, *out of* in the walking sentence is a different verb, *kumútu*, which means "exit":

Mi wáka kumútu a dí wósu. "I walked out of the house."

The difference is that you push something, but you don't walk something, you just walk.* *Push* is transitive, *walk* is intransitive. What determines whether you use *púu* or *kumútu* with a verb in Saramaccan is that distinction. We're a long way from languages like Pashto, where you can't do anything with a verb without attending to whether it's transitive, but still—language is intricate, even when it didn't exist until William Shakespeare was decades gone and New York City already existed.

Meanwhile, Saramaccan is an *oral* rather than written language. But what's interesting is that among the few Saramaka who have reason to write it much, there are already tendencies, inherited from traditions of writing European languages, to "unravel" things like unaccented pronouns. In the airport drinking sentence in Saramaccan, *it* is the unaccented third person pronoun, ế:

Mi	sá	bebé	ế	kabá	akí	ɔ́?
I	can	drink	it	finish	here	QU

"Can I drink it here?"

In e-mails, however, one of my consultants on the language writes ế as the full, accented form *hế* out of a natural sense that it is a more careful version of ế. Which, at first, it surely was. But now it's a new form, period. No one would ever actually use *hế* in this way unless they wanted to say, "Well, what about this one? Can I drink *IT* here?" which is not the sort of thing my consultant has meant in the sentences he writes. As always, writing is an approximation, dance chart–style, of what we actually do when we speak.

What do you get, then, when you throw together words from five languages and grammar from two? If anyone has to speak it for long, what you get is a language—very much an

---

* Indeed, you can walk a dog or walk a mile, but these are secondary definitions, different "entries" in our mental lexicon from the basic conception. In terms of the simple act of walking, you just walk—maybe *to a bus stop* or *in a hurry*, but these aren't objects.

IDIOM in the sense of all of the others we have seen in this book. Even a language born as a train wreck between a bunch of languages rises again and remains a language indeed.

This is only an extreme manifestation of a generality. Languages are always impure. There are too many of them on this small planet for any one of them to have remained only itself.

THIS VIEW OF LANGUAGE

I began this book by comparing the typical view of the languages of the world to aquatic creatures moldering on beaches and on the margins of illustrations in crumbling old books. If a lake were drained of water and we were presented with the creatures left behind gasping on their way to expiration as a useful picture of Our Underwater Friends, we would find it, at the very least, homely. The same judgment applies to the way we tend to be presented with what language is like.

This is: Of all of the languages in the world, a certain few are "real." They are mostly spoken on the peninsula that we call Europe, including their renditions spread elsewhere starting in the fifteenth century, American English being one of them. Then if pressed as to what some other "real" languages are, we would throw in Chinese, Japanese, Korean, Arabic, Hebrew, Persian, and probably Hindi. Other languages—including ones spoken by as many people as Swahili, Indonesian, and the Philippines' Tagalog—are "tongues," "idioms," "dialects," "whatever it is that he speaks," probably not as complicated as ours.

Plus even with a "real" language, you can barely shake a stick without hitting someone who doesn't speak it "right." Or mixes it up with something else. Language, from this perspective, is like the rock that Sisyphus rolled eternally up the hill but never quite made it—two steps back for every step forward.

Although we don't think of it this way, our sense of language stipulates that almost every human on earth is either speaking something primitive or speaking something wrong.

If there was grandeur in Darwin's view of life, there is certainly nothing grand in that glum view of language. It neglects so much beauty and so much complexity. And luckily, it's inaccurate.

The reason I have shown you things in such a wide and even weird variety of languages (Archi? Keo?) is to get across how language looks to people who have fallen into the odd circumstance of studying it as a career. It filters how we read what is said about languages in the newspaper, how we hear what people say about languages in passing, and how we perceive languages themselves when we hear them spoken, including our own.

Under this view of language, "a language" in the generic sense is more complicated than English or other ones Americans tend to be most familiar with. Most languages that die were interesting not just in having picturesque idioms, but in that while children grew up speaking them effortlessly, for us to even learn to produce good basic sentences in them, we would have had to apply the kind of concentration usually reserved for Differential Quotients or *Moby-Dick*.

What's unusual is not when a language is frighteningly complicated, but when it isn't.* That is, the almost willfully opaque quality of Navajo is almost less interesting, in the scientific sense, than the queer simplicity of Flores languages like Keo.

Complexity in language is about more than endings. It's about tones, classifiers, transitive versus intransitive, ways of

---

* Properly speaking, this part about small languages being more complex is more My View of Language, as well as that of what began as a scattering of linguists who came to think that way independently and started corresponding about ten years ago. There is now a growing coterie of linguists of various stripes studying the issue, and from the combined impact of conferences, anthology volumes, and citations, I feel safe in assuming that this basic perspective is becoming an accepted generalization.

indicating that something landed, expressive particles, and much else. A language is not complex only, or even mainly, in the extent to which learning it requires memorizing tables of suffixes. That is just one game plan a language can follow, a Eurasian fetish, as arbitrary and peculiar as the game plan of Akha and Chinese, with their tones and particles. If someone were to build a language from the ground up, it would not have tones like Akha giving five meanings to the same little syllable, but it wouldn't have tables of endings like Spanish either—as creole languages like Saramaccan show us.

The way any language is now is one of endless possibilities that have resulted from drift over millennia, not what the heart of language must be. What would be interesting is if there were a language that started as a pidgin, developed on its own, and came out just a few hundred years later looking like Pashto. Or if all or even most of the world's languages worked more or less like Latin—or Chinese.

To linguists, writing is not what language is, and a language is not less of one because it isn't written down. Our default sense of language, in fact, is an oral "tongue" its speakers consider odd to see on the page. Writing is aesthetically pleasing and certainly useful, but language started as something spoken, and speaking remains the way the vast bulk of language is produced. Much of the sense that a dialect like Black English is "bad grammar" and Colloquial Sinhalese is "not a language" is due to the fact that tradition has largely kept them from the printed page. Yet it is the page that harbors a less "real" rendition of language than the mouth.

A linguist expects that if a language has a healthy population of speakers, then there will likely be nonstandard dialects of it commonly thought of as "mistaken" when they are actually full-blown, nuanced speech just as the standard is. The typical evaluation of Black English is paralleled not only by that of colloquial Indonesian, but by that of "Pidgin" in Hawaii, urban varieties of widespread African languages like Wolof, Hausa, and Swahili, and countless other speech varieties worldwide.

The evaluation is understandable but inappropriate; we shake our heads.

Mixture can also inform that evaluation. On languages of Africa, for example, a Senegalese man speaking Serer, a relative of that country's main African lingua franca, Wolof, once rued to me that young Serer men in Dakar were speaking something "not Serer." It turned out that they were sprinkling their Serer with a lot of French and a few American hip-hop words. But their effortless control of Serer's *ten genders* (!!)* made what they were speaking Serer indeed. All languages are mixed to an extent, and even a language most of whose original words have been replaced by foreign ones remains, because of its grammar, itself. English is an example: in that last sentence, *language*, *mix*, *extent*, *original*, *replace*, *foreign*, *remain*, and *grammar* are all borrowed from French and would have been alien to an Old English speaker.[†] Yet whatever you think of my compositional skills in English (too "oral" for many, I know—sorry), if I'm writing in French just now, it is surely the most flabbergastingly inept, ungrammatical French ever attempted in the two millennia or so of the language's existence.

Then, even a language that is part one *grammar* and part another one (or two, or three) is not less of a language—it's just one more language. An island like Sri Lanka is home to not just two written standard languages but three unwritten mulatto ones—and that's just on a button of terra firma the size of West Virginia. Imagine the true language situation in South Africa, China (Wutun was but a tiny hint), or India, replete with ample dialects of each language plus mixtures, pidgins, creoles, and assorted intermediate cases.

In the scientific sense, then, Spanglish is not "interesting."

---

* That is, ten classes that nouns can fit into. There are four plural "classes," too, but they involve the same basic ten categorizations. In any case, marking these classes is about both prefixes *and* suffixes. Language hurts.

† Plus: I did not craft that sentence to deliberately tilt it toward French. I only decided to point out the Frenchness of it during revisions after the first draft.

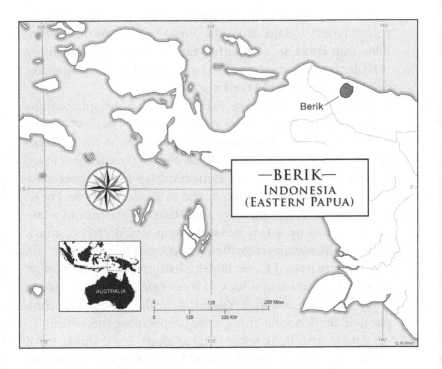

—BERIK—
INDONESIA
(EASTERN PAPUA)

That is, although surely it is a rich source of cultural analysis, no linguist considers it unexpected that a Spanish with a heavy overlay of English words would exist among, well, Spanish speakers in an English-speaking country! What would be interesting is if there were no Spanglish. In that vein, for example, it is *interesting* that despite Brazil's plantation history, there is apparently no truly creole Portuguese spoken there along the lines of Saramaccan or Haitian. You would expect one, yet it is absent. The linguist is perplexed; the linguist is intrigued.

HERE'S WHAT I MEAN BY interesting. Of the several hundred languages spoken on the island of New Guinea, one is called Berik. About fifteen hundred people speak it, a group of people largely isolated from the outside world until the 1970s. Bible translators spent twenty years with the Berik, learning their language from the ground up. So what kind of language would a people like the Berik speak?

Certainly, it will have expressions and metaphors quite unlike anything Westerners are used to. The "money" factoid on Berik is that to them, the soul happens to be in the gall bladder. *Nice to see you* in Berik is *My gall bladder is really warm today*.

But as bracing as this is, alone it implies that languages are different only in terms of words and expressions. It would be so easy to suppose, gall bladders aside, that the *grammar* of a language spoken by a tiny isolated group wouldn't need much structure. It was never written down until recently, after all. The Berik marveled to see Bible translators taking down what they said and reading it back to them before they were able to really speak the language. Russian is "real," "developed," complicated. Berik is some thing some people speak somewhere.

And at first, Berik tempts that analysis. You'd think that if there's one thing a language would need, it would be six pronouns for the first, second, and third persons in the singular and the plural. You know: Spanish's *yo, tú, él, nosotros, vosotros, ellos*, plus the feminine versions of the third person ones, *ella* and *ellas*. But a first clue that this isn't necessary is, of all languages, English—we use *you* in the singular *and* plural. Berik takes that further: only in the first person is there a plural pronoun *we*. Otherwise, not only does Berik have no plural for *you*, but it doesn't have one for *he/she* either—the same word, *je*, means *he, she, it*, and *they*.

"Primitive." But then, as if it has just been being coy, Berik comes out and hits you right between the eyes. Berik verbs are some of the most ingrown on the planet. Person and number? That's Berik baby food. A proper verb in this tiny language must also specify things like how big an object is, whether there was one, two, or three of them, whether it's high or low, how far away it was, and the specific time of day! *Kitobana* means "gives three big things to a man in the sunlight" while *golbifi*—the same verb root, with different decorations—means "will give one big thing to a woman in the dark." "Put a big thing down low nearby" is *gwerantena*. The same *put* verb, but referring to putting that big thing up high way over there, is *tosonswetna*.

Here's a language that has clearly not suffered the slings and arrows of adults learning it. It has inched its way into requiring a marker for an endless number of nuances of living that no language needs, yet that a language can happily schlepp along with forever with no detriment to children or their parents. Recall the senseless complexity of Ket, the grades of *very* indexed to individual adjectives in Akha, and the nonexistence of the regular verb in Navajo. This endless elaboration slows down or stops only if something happens to get in its way. Usually nothing does.

Ironically, the majestic complexity of a Berik is what makes it normal. Therein lies the grandeur in This View of Language.

NOTES ON SOURCES

INTRODUCTION

Undersea illustration back in the day: Inspired by the essay "Seeing Eye to Eye, Through a Glass Clearly" in Stephen Jay Gould, *Leonardo's Mountain of Clams and the Diet of Worms* (New York: Three Rivers, 1998).

Nasioi: William Foley, *The Papuan Languages of New Guinea* (Cambridge: Cambridge University Press, 1986), pp. 83–85.

Lederer book: Richard Lederer, *Crazy English* (New York: Pocket Books, 1989).

The perfectly pleasant article: Ellen Barry, "In Dagestan, Laugh Track Echoes Across Mountains," *New York Times*, February 16, 2010.

Johanna Nichols, "The Nakh-Daghestanian Consonant Correspondences," *Current Trends in Caucasian, East European and Inner Asian Linguistics*, ed. by Dee Ann Holisky and Kevin Tuite (Amsterdam: John Benjamins, 2003), pp. 207–51.

Pei: Mario Pei, *The Story of Language* (Philadelphia: Lippincott, 1949).

Article in *Language*: P. Haupt, "The Influence of Caucasian Idioms on Indo-European Languages," *Language* 1 (1925): pp. 14–18.

On the Archi double consonants: Archi experts indicate this kind of sound by writing the consonant once, followed by a kind of semicolon, but I am doing a more meat-and-potatoes double consonant for clarity to people beyond that tiny club. A. E. Kibrik, "Archi," in *Handbook of Morphology*, ed. by Andrew Spencer and Arnold Zwick (Oxford: Blackwell, 1998), pp. 455–76.

CHAPTER ONE

Pashto samples: D. N. MacKenzie, "Pashto," in *The World's Major Languages*, ed. by Bernard Comrie (New York: Oxford, 1987), pp. 547–65.

Persian samples: Gernot L. Windfuhr, "Persian," in *The World's Major Languages*, ed. by Bernard Comrie (New York: Oxford, 1987), pp. 523–46.

Old Persian: Benjamin W. Fortson IV, *Indo-European Language and Culture* (Maldon, MA: Wiley-Blackwell, 2010), p. 240.

Demography in Persia: Richard N. Frye, *The Heritage of Persia* (Cleveland: World Publishing Co., 1963), p. 96; Josef Wiesehöfer, *Ancient Persia from 550 BC to 650 AD* (London: I. B. Tauris, 1996), p. 78; J. M. Cook, *The Persian Empire* (New York: Schocken, 1983), p. 87.

M17 distribution in Iran: Spencer Wells et al., "The Eurasian Heartland: A Continental Perspective on Y-Chromosome Diversity," *Proceedings of the National Academy of Sciences* 98 (2001).

Mandarin classifier etymologies: Jerry Norman, *Chinese* (Cambridge: Cambridge University Press, 1988), pp. 115–16.

Cantonese classifiers: Stephen Matthews and Virginia Yip, *Cantonese: A Comprehensive Grammar* (London: Routledge, 1994), pp. 102–4.

Nasioi classifiers: William Foley, *The Papuan Languages of New Guinea* (Cambridge: Cambridge University Press, 1986), p. 84.

Kikuyu and Yupik direction words: J. Peter Denny, "Locating the Universal in Lexical Systems for Spatial Deixis," *Papers from the Parasession on the Lexicon*, ed. by Donka Farkas, Wesley M. Jacobsen, and Karol W. Todrys (Chicago: Chicago Linguistics Society, 1978), pp. 71–84.

Muna: René van den Berg, *A Grammar of the Muna Language* (Dordrecht-Holland: Foris, 1989), pp. 89–90.

Moroccan Arabic history: My main sources are J. M. Abun-Nasr, *A History of the Maghrib in the Islamic Period* (Cambridge: Cambridge University Press, 1987), and Kees Versteegh, *The Arabic Language* (New York: Columbia University Press, 1997).

Haitian Creole sentence: Ralph Ludwig, Sylviane Telchid, and Florence Bruneau-Ludwig, *Corpus créole* eds., (Hamburg: Helmut Buske, 2001), p. 164.

Ket: "I come," "I go," and "I go to the river" sentences from Edward J. Vajda, "Yeniseic diathesis," *Linguistic Typology* 9 (2005): 327–39. My description of the function of the two sets of pronoun prefixes is also based on Vajda's analysis. Other Ket data and descriptions are from Heinrich Werner, *Die Ketische Sprache* (Wiesbaden: Harrasso-witz, 1997).

Tukang Besi: Mark Donohue, *A Grammar of Tukang Besi* (Berlin: Mouton de Gruyter, 1999), p. 297.

Leti: Aone Van Engelenhoven, *Leti: A Language of Southwest Maluku* (Leiden: KITLV Press, 2004), p. 235.

Keo: Louise Baird, *A Grammar of Kéo: A Language of East Nusantara* (Australian National University PhD dissertation, 2002), p. 491.

Ngadha: P. Arndt, *Grammatik der Ngad'a Sprache*. Bandung: A. C. Nix. (Verhandelingen: Koninklijk Bataviaasche Genootschap van Kun-sten en Wetenschappen 72:3).

Ende: Bradley J. McDonnell, "Possessive Structures in Ende: A Language of Eastern Indonesia," paper presented at Tenth International Con-ference on Austronesian Linguistics, January 2006, Puerto Princesa City, Philippines.

Neat paper that asks "why?": Gary Lupyan and Rick Dale, "Language Structure Is Partly Determined by Social Structure," *PloS One* 5:1 (2010).

Wray and Grace: Alison Wray and George W. Grace, "The Consequences of Talking to Strangers: Evolutionary Corollaries of Socio-Cultural Influences on Linguistics Form," *Lingua* 117 (2007): 543–78.

CHAPTER TWO

Ket relationship with Navajo: The closest source to handy at present is *The Dene-Yeniseian Connection,* (University of Alaska, Fairbanks & Native Language Center, 2010).

Navajo: My presentation of Navajo is based mostly on data from Leon-ard Faltz, *The Navajo Verb* (Albuquerque: University of New Mexico Press, 1998), supplemented by some from Robert W. Young and Wil-liam Morgan, *The Navajo Language: A Grammar and Colloquial Dic-tionary* (Albuquerque: University of New Mexico Press, 1987). This latter is the book I ran up against as a graduate student.

Sensitivity to shape among Navajo, white, and black children: The most accessible account is in John A. Lucy, *Language Diversity and Thought* (Cambridge: Cambridge University Press, 1992), pp. 198–200.

Mandarin classifier etymologies: Jerry Norman, *Chinese* (Cambridge: Cambridge University Press, 1988), pp. 115–16.

CHAPTER THREE

Comment on difficulty of Ghanaian languages: William (Willem) Bosman, *A New and Accurate Description of the Coast of Guinea* (London: James Knapton, 1705), p. 131.

Asante material: Florence Abena Dolphyne, *The Akan (Twi-Fante) Language: Its Sound Systems and Tonal Structure* (Accra: Ghana Universities Press, 1988), pp. 68–71.

Von Humboldt quote: Wilhelm von Humboldt, *On Language,* ed. by Michael Losonsky (Cambridge: Cambridge University Press, 1999), p. 206–7.

Akha material: Inga-Lill Hansson, "Akha," in *The Sino-Tibetan Languages,* ed. by Graham Thurgood and Randy J. LaPolla (London: Routledge, 2003), pp. 236–51.

Shirley story: This was distributed in the California State Department of Education's *Lesson Plan Handbook* for the Proficiency in Standard English for Speakers of Black Language program starting in 1981. This handbook was not sold to the public, and I am not aware of the author of the passage (but admire their dead-on ear for the dialect).

Fongbe material: Claire Lefebvre and Anne-Marie Brousseau, *A Grammar of Fongbe* (Berlin: Mouton de Gruyter, 2001).

People identifying speakers as black over the phone: Guy Bailey and Natalie Maynor, "The Divergence Controversy," *American Speech* 64: 12–39; John Baugh, "Perceptions Within a Variable Paradigm: Black and White Racial Detection and Identification Based on Speech," *Focus on the U.S.A.,* ed. by Edgar Schneider (Amsterdam: John Benjamins, 1996), pp. 169–82.

Consonant clusters in Black English: Walt Wolfram and Ralph Fasold, *The Study of Social Dialects in American English* (Englewood Cliffs, NJ: Prentice Hall, 1974), p. 134.

Aramaic material: Otto Jastrow, "The Neo-Aramaic Languages," in *The Semitic Languages,* ed. by Robert Hetzron (New York: Oxford University Press, 1997), pp. 334–77.

Zuckerman argument: Most usefully put forth in Ghil'ad Zuckerman, "Hybridity versus Revivability: Multiple Causation, Forms and Patterns," *Journal of Language Contact VARIA* 2: 40–67.

Black English and *ass*: All sentences (including the malformed ones) plus information on other languages from Chris Collins, Simanique Moody, and Paul M. Postal, "An AAE Camouflage Construction," *Language* 84 (2008): 29–68.

CHAPTER FOUR

Leti pronouns: Aone Van Engelenhoven, *Leti: A Language of Southwest Maluku* (Leiden: KITLV Press, 2004), p. 149.

Indonesian sentences with *men-* and *di-*: D. J. Prentice, D. J. Malay (Indonesian and Malaysian), *The World's Major Languages*, ed. by Bernard Comrie (New York: Oxford University Press, 1987), p. 933. Prentice translated the sentences with *strike*; I substituted *hit* because it sounds more natural, particularly in American English.

Comparison of standard and Jakartan Indonesian sentences: Thanks to David Gil.

Sinhalese material: James W. Gair, *Studies in South Asian Linguistics* (New York: Oxford University Press, 1998), pp. 17, 213–67.

Riau Indonesian sentences: David Gil, "The Prefixes *di-* and *N-* in Malay/Indonesian Dialects," in *Voice in the Languages of Nusa Tenggara Barat*, ed. by Fay Wouk and Malcolm Ross (Canberra: Pacific Linguistics, 2002), pp. 241–83.

Abau language lessons: Donald Laycock, "Multilingualism: Linguistic Boundaries and Unsolved Problems in Papua New Guinea," in *New Guinea and Neighboring Areas: A Sociolinguistic Laboratory*, ed. by Stephen A. Wurm (The Hague: Mouton De Gruyter, 1979), pp. 81–99.

CHAPTER FIVE

Wutun: Mei W. Lee-Smith and Stephen A. Wurm, "The Wutun Language," in *Atlas of Languages of Intercultural Communication in the Pacific, Asia, and the Americas* (Volume II.2), ed. by Stephen A. Wurm, Peter Mühlhäusler, and Darrell T. Tryon (Berlin: Mouton de Gruyter, 1996), pp. 883–97.

Nigerian Pidgin: Nicholas Faraclas, *Nigerian Pidgin* (London: Routledge, 1996). The language, for the record, is one of several that are popularly called "pidgin" but which are actually full-grown new languages (e.g., creoles).

Ghanaian Pidgin English: The authoritative source is Magnus Huber, *Ghanaian Pidgin English in Its West African Context* (Amsterdam: John Benjamins, 1999). See the citation of Nigerian Pidgin above on the "pidgin" appellation of this language.

Sri Lanka Portuguese: Ian R. Smith, "The Development of Morphosyntax in Sri Lanka Portuguese," in *York Papers in Linguistics 11*, ed. by Mark Sebba and Loreto Todd (York: University of York, 1984), pp. 291–301; John Holm, *Pidgins and Creoles* (Vol. II) (Cambridge: Cambridge University Press, 1989), p. 290.

Sri Lanka Malay: Sebastian Nordhoff, *A Grammar of Upcountry Sri Lanka Malay* (Utrecht: LOT, 2009), pp. 334, 569.

Sinhalese versus Tamil influence on Sri Lanka Malay: Umberto Ansaldo, "Sri Lanka Malay Revised: Genesis and Classification," in *A World of Many Voices: Lessons from Documented Endangered Languages*, ed. by A. Dwyer, D. Harrison, and D. Rood (Amsterdam: John Benjamins, 2008), pp. 13–42.

Vedda data: K. N. O. Dharmadasa, "The Creolization of an Aboriginal Language: The Case of Vedda in Sri Lanka (Ceylon)," *Anthropological Linguistics* 16: 79–106.

Saramaccan: Well, for the most part I just know because I've been studying it for twenty years. There is no single go-to source. If you want to know more about the people, then I recommend Richard Price and Sally Price, *Two Evenings in Saramaka* (Chicago: University of Chicago Press, 1991); this is one of several books the Prices, anthropologists who lived long-term among the Saramaka, have published both together and separately, and you can use the *Two Evenings* book for references to the others. For the Saramaka's history, you have to go to a university library and look at Richard Price, *The Guiana Maroons: A Historical and Bibliographical Introduction* (Baltimore: Johns Hopkins University Press, 1976). The history of the language was most conclusively nailed by Morris Goodman in "The Portuguese Element in the American Creoles," in *Pidgin and Creole Languages*, ed. by Glenn G. Gilbert (Honolulu: University of Hawaii Press, 1987), pp. 361–405. Beware any claim you encounter that Saramaccan is a continuation of a worldwide maritime Portuguese pidgin, an idea that seemed plausible on the basis of what was known thirty years ago but which no working specialist on the topic subscribes to today, although sources by innocent laymen sometimes continue to repeat it as fact. On the grammar of the language itself, in this book I am using data from what some guy named John McWhorter will be publishing in a collection of his articles, which at this writing is to be titled *Linguistic Simplicity and Complexity: Why Languages Undress* (Berlin: Mouton de Gruyter, 2011), and after that in a grammatical description of Saramaccan with Jeff Good, which will be published not long afterward.

EPILOGUE

Berik material: For pronouns, Michael Cysouw, *The Paradigmatic Structure of Person Marking* (New York: Oxford University, 2003); for verbs, Peter Westrum, "A Grammatical Sketch of Berik," *Irian* 16 (1988): 133–87; also, there is now this podcast (my first time writing *that* word) describing the language's documentation and some facts about it (five kinds of *l*!): http://www.theworld.org/tag/berik/.

ACKNOWLEDGMENTS

There are things that only a few people on the planet know. There were occasions while writing this book that such people came to my aid on information of that kind. They were Greville Corbett (Archi), Johanna Nichols (Northeast Caucasian history), and David Gil (for the direct contrast between a standard and colloquial Indonesian sentence of just the kind that he knew I "meant"). I am also deeply grateful to Geoffrey Hull for giving me sources a while back on the vocabulary of deeply obscure Eastern Indonesian languages, which I would never have come across otherwise, and to two of my Saramaccan consultants, Rohit Paulus and Gerda Menig, who have been the sources since 2001 of most of the Saramaccan sentences in Chapter Five.

There are things that only some people will allow. I salute my agent Katinka Matson and, at Gotham Books, William Shinker, Patrick Mulligan, and Travers Johnson for working with me yet again on a book that surely looked a little odd in proposal form.

There are things that only some people can do. I am not among those to whom book titles come easily. Endless gratitude to Harold Itzkowitz for the title of this one—and after fifteen seconds of looking through the galleys, no less.

INDEX

Page numbers in *italics* refer to illustrations.

ALSO BY JOHN McWHORTER

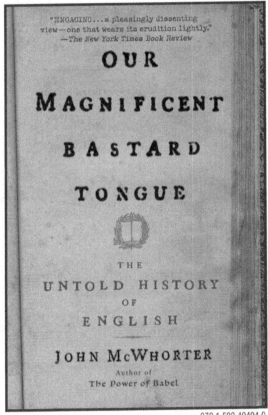

"ENGAGING...a pleasingly dissenting
view—one that wears its erudition lightly."
—*The New York Times Book Review*

OUR

MAGNIFICENT

BASTARD

TONGUE

THE
UNTOLD HISTORY
OF
ENGLISH

JOHN McWHORTER
Author of
The Power of Babel

978-1-592-40494-0

New York Times bestselling author and renowned linguist John McWhorter
explores the quirks and quandaries of the English language,
focusing on our strange and wonderful grammar.

AVAILABLE NOW FROM

Printed in the United States
by Baker & Taylor Publisher Services